This book belongs to...

_____

A Woman's Guide to Making Right Choices

ELIZABETH GEORGE

HARVEST HOUSE PUBLISHER
EUGENE, OREGON

Cover by Dugan Design Group, Bloomington, Minnesota

Cover photos © Fotostudio FM / Corbis Bridge / Alamy; Tetra Images / Alamy; iStockphoto / Marinamik

A WOMAN'S GUIDE TO MAKING RIGHT CHOICES
Copyright © 2012 by Elizabeth George
Published by Harvest House Publishers
Eugene, Oregon 97402
www.harvesthousepublishers.com

ISBN 978-0-7369-5118-0 (pbk.)
ISBN 978-0-7369-5119-7 (eBook)

Printed in the United States of America

12 13 14 15 16 17 18 19 20 / LB-KBD / 10 9 8 7 6 5 4 3 2 1

Contents

1

Life Is Full of Choices

*Mary has chosen that good part,
which will not be taken away from her.*
—Luke 10:42

id you get it? Did you get it?" came my husband's rapid-fire questions even before he was halfway in the door after work.

"Get what?" I innocently replied as I stopped from working on our dinner to greet him.

"Did you get your letter?"

"What letter?" (I wasn't sure how much longer I could keep up this act of feigned ignorance. After all, we did get more than one letter that day.)

"The letter from the church. About the new women's ministry."

"Ooooh, *that* letter."

"So what do you think? Are you going to be a part of it? Did you sign it?"

"Well…I threw it in the trash. I just don't think teaching is my thing. I'm sure there are many more women who could do a much better job of teaching the Bible. And you as a pastor should know that the Bible says, 'Let not many of you become teachers, knowing that we shall receive a stricter judgment' (James 3:1)."

Well, this is a little of the scene that transpired in our kitchen as Jim and I discussed the letter I received from the leadership board at our church. It announced the formation of a new women's ministry, and to kick things off, asked if any of the leaders' wives would be willing to conduct an elective workshop.

Jim, ever the positive encourager—make that *super*-positive encourager!—gingerly picked through the trash to retrieve the letter and smoothed it out on the kitchen countertop. He smiled as he sweetly reminded me that I had been studying what I called "the pink passages" in the Bible for the past ten years. His final salvo shot across my resistant bow: "Don't you think that, after all these years of studying the women of the Bible, you just might have something to say on the subject?"

Well, with that reality check and its stewardship hanging over my head, I had a serious choice to make. Would I choose to give in to my fears and decline this opportunity, or would I choose to trust God to somehow see me through the ordeal I suspected it would be?

Well, to finish the story, I did choose to teach a class on the women of the Bible. To my relief, there were only six women who enrolled for this elective. I was so thrilled! This I could handle. I went around the house for *days* saying, "Thank You, Lord! Oh, thank You, Lord!" My six new friends and I sat around in a circle and had an incredible time together week after week. And did I ever continue to thank God for His mercy!

Then, as the semester of the new women's Bible studies was nearing its end, I got another letter. It, too, began, "Dear leader's wife…" This time the board was asking me and the other women who had taught classes to pray about repeating our electives. So, having made the initial choice to teach, I agreed. But this time, 60 women signed up. This was *totally* unexpected for me—60 women? This meant rather than a small, cozy setting, things would have to be more formal—a lectern, a microphone, a classroom. But I bit the bullet and I made it through just one more time…or so I thought!

Then I received a third letter: "Dear leader's wife…" (As I read this I thought, *By this time don't you think someone would know our names? After all, here we are serving the church, helping this new ministry to take off!*) This letter, as you've probably guessed, asked if I would be willing to teach my elective a third time so those who hadn't been able to attend it yet could have another chance.

Well, I just knew I couldn't possibly end up with more than 60 women in the class, so I said yes. Now, before I say what happened, realize that Jim and I were members of a church of 10,000 people. As it turned out, 600 women showed up, so we had to move my group into the church auditorium. All I can say is thank goodness God is faithful not to give us more than we can handle (1 Corinthians 10:13)! Whew!

The point of all this is not the size of the class or the number of people. Rather, my point is that I made a choice to step out in faith, to trust God, to set myself and my fears aside, and to concentrate on others. God honored this choice. That one reluctant choice made by a reluctant servant of the Lord ended up launching my teaching and writing ministry. Who knew?! Least of all, not me!

Your Life Is Full of Choices

Now, you might be thinking, *I'm glad I don't have to make that kind of choice! Teaching the Bible is definitely not my gift!* But what about having to choose how to educate your children—

home school, private Christian school, or public school? Or what about figuring out how to care for a parent who has dementia—in your home, in a sibling's home, in a nursing home? On and on the list of your choices goes. And it often seems like the decisions you need to make are bombarding your door before you even get out of bed each day!

As we begin putting together some guidelines for making right choices, you already know that life is full of choices. In fact, you had to make a choice to even start reading this book about how to make decisions! So, the issue is not the mere act of making choices itself, but rather learning how to make not just good choices, or better choices, but the best choices.

Here are a few thoughts about the nature of making choices that will help get us started:

Choices always result in consequences. Recently my husband was reading a book titled *How to Ruin Your Life by 40*, by Steve Farrar.[1] In the very first chapter we are introduced to an 18-year-old woman named Jane. She had just lost her husband. She had no support of any kind, and was the mother of two small children. Destitute, she went to a bluff overlooking a lake with the very real thought of jumping and ending her life.

The story went on to relate how this distraught young woman's attention ended up being diverted by something on the other side of the lake. With this break to her dark thoughts, she chose to turn around, leave the lake, and return home. Now, nothing had changed. Her life still seemed hopeless. But a few weeks after this experience at the lake, Jane came to faith in Christ. Later she met and married Captain John Guinness, whose great-great-grandson is Os Guinness, a well-known Christian apologist and author of more than 20 books.

This is how Farrar concludes this story of Jane Guinness:

She [Jane] had a choice to make, and that choice would carry consequences.

That concept is known as cause and effect.

With the wrong choice she could have ruined her life and her future. With the wrong choice she would ruin the childhood of her young children.

But she made the right choice as an eighteen-year-old. And her family is still grateful today that she did, nearly two hundred years later.

The choices you are making in your life are just as significant.[2]

Choices are not always of equal value. Obviously, the choice Jane made was of great value. It was a life-and-death choice. Many choices you make are more everyday in nature, like what to wear to a party or shower, or which cereal to eat for breakfast. But every now and then you are faced with more serious and potentially life-changing choices, such as which career to pursue, or whether or not to marry. Because you don't know in advance how the vital choice you make in a single day will impact your life, you want to make sure you handle each choice with care, and call upon God for wisdom and guidance.

Choices happen by default. The fact that you keep putting off going to see the doctor about your persistent pain is actually a choice. You are afraid of what the pain might represent, so you keep delaying the call. Waiting to make a decision is not always bad, but in this case, a delay could mean the difference between life or death. When we feel uncomfortable about a choice, we sometimes delay in doing what is right, just, fair, or edifying—like asking someone for forgiveness.

At other times we delay because we are just lazy or we don't think the matter is all that important…or it's going to take soooo much time! Take a simple choice like reading your Bible. You can say, "I don't have time to read my Bible." So you don't. But in reality, if you were honest with yourself, you would admit you are actually saying, "I'm choosing not to read my Bible."

Choices have only two outcomes. Choices are either good or bad. Right or wrong. And half of a wrong choice—or a partially wrong choice—is still a wrong choice.

My favorite example is, "I'll do that later." While I might have all the good intentions of doing the right thing and making the right choice, what usually happens is my partially wrong choice to do it later leads to and blossoms into a full-out wrong choice when I don't get around to doing it at all!

Recognizing there are only two outcomes helps make decision-making a clearer process for you. When you are faced with a choice to make, either do it or don't do it—right now. And if you know there is something extremely important you need to do to benefit others, then do it right now.

Choices are often made due to the influence of others. You cannot escape the fact that you are constantly being influenced in your choices. Your environment, your culture, your family, your friends, your fears, your pride, your greed—all of these external forces are bearing down heavily upon you.

God's solution? Surround yourself with as many positive influences as possible. Otherwise, the apostle Paul's observation will always prove true and win out: "Do not be deceived: 'Bad company corrupts good morals'" (1 Corinthians 15:33 NASB).

Choices made correctly will require forethought. The book of Proverbs repeatedly warns against making hasty decisions, and calls those people who rush into trouble "fools" (Proverbs 13:16).

What can you do? Delay your decisions as long as you can. This will help you make as close to the right decision as possible based on time—time spent praying, time spent seeking the Bible's direction, and time spent listening to wise counsel.

Choices made correctly will put you in the center of God's will. God's perfect will always comes with right choices. This is why it is so important to study God's Word, pray, and seek godly counsel. "As you have always obeyed…work out your own salvation with fear and trembling; for it is God who works in you both to will and to do for His good pleasure" (Philippians 2:12-13).

> ### A Few More Things to Remember About Choices
> —Attractive choices sometimes lead to sin.
> —Good choices have positive long-term results.
> —Right choices are sometimes difficult.[3]

Looking at Choices Through the Rearview Mirror

Let's focus for a moment. Earlier I said that choices always have a consequence. For me, when I volunteered to teach my first class, the consequence was having to study, prepare, and stand in front of all those women and pray like crazy with every breath that my mind and mouth would work…and my legs wouldn't collapse! It was a frightening consequence at first, but in time— with the Lord's help!—I gained some priceless experience, and I learned better to deal with the demands and my fears.

You've probably been to a women's retreat or attended Bible study where there was a time for the women to share with one another, a time when they would talk about choices they had made in their past. In a sense it's as if they were looking at their past in a rearview mirror and seeing all over again what had happened to them.

Well, all I can say is, "Praise the Lord, God did some major healing in the lives of those precious women. Thank God they are no longer living back in their past." But, at the same time, they can still see, remember, taste, and relive the consequences of their actions. Sometimes their language includes phrases like…

> I wandered off the path…
> I became like the prodigal son…
> I fell away from the Lord…
> I got sidetracked in sin…
> I lost my first love…
> I strayed from the truth…
> I made some wrong decisions…
> I went off the deep end…
> I got in with the wrong crowd…

As you've listened to the stories during such sharing sessions, have you ever found yourself wondering, *What happened? How does someone wander off the path, lose their first love for Jesus, stray from the truth, fall off the deep end, or get involved with the wrong crowd?*

Well, we both know what happened, don't we? Somehow, at some time, for some reason, a wrong choice was made. Maybe it was just a little lie. Just a little lack of concern for what was right. Just a little bending of a rule. Then little by little these lesser yet wrong choices became bigger and easier…until one day a woman finally realizes her life has become a mess.

Women of the Bible and Their Choices

I don't know about you, but it comforts me and gives me solid assurance to *know* that the Bible is always relevant to my challenges as a woman. It is filled—and overflowing!—with God's wisdom and 100 percent guaranteed guidance. And it never fails to offer help for the many choices you and I are facing today. Here's what I'm talking about!

Eve made a choice—Literally right from the beginning of biblical history, Eve, the mother of all women, was faced with a choice. You are probably familiar with this part of Eve's story, the first woman on earth and the wife of Adam (see Genesis 3:1-6). This woman was asked by the evil serpent to choose to do her own thing and eat some beautiful, delicious-looking fruit because doing so would make a person smart. To make such a choice meant she had to make a choice to disobey God, who had forbidden Adam and Eve from eating of that particular tree's fruit.

Well, the whole world is still reeling from Eve's wrong choice. She ate! Never mind God. Never mind her husband. Never mind the consequences that are still reverberating down through all of time. Never mind the marring of her future offspring. Eve wanted what Eve wanted—and Eve ate.

Lot's wife made a choice—Don't even get me started about her husband, Lot! Ohhhh! He chose—yes, chose—to move his family and possessions to the green valley of Sodom and Gomorrah, which just happened to be the two most evil cities of his day (Genesis 13:10-11).

The sad result of Lot's flirtation with the world came when God sent two angels to save Lot and his family before God brought destruction on these wicked cities and their people. The angels distinctly warned Lot and his wife to not look back at the city. That's pretty clear, right? But evidently the lure of the "big city lifestyle" was too much for Mrs. Lot and she looked back. She willfully made a wrong choice and it cost her her life as she was turned instantly into a pillar of salt (Genesis 19:26).

Mary made a choice—Can you remember how silly you were as a young teen, back when you were 15 years old? Well, this is not how we find young Mary in Luke 1:26-38. When confronted by the angel Gabriel and told of her opportunity to become the human mother of God's Son, she could have declined. You see, she was betrothed to a wonderful man named Joseph. She knew one consequence of choosing to accept God's will for her would mean an instant dissolution of her engagement.

What did Mary do? She chose to trust God. And I just adore the words in her acceptance speech: "Behold the maidservant of the Lord! Let it be to me according to your word" (verse 38).

Another Mary made a choice—Who is the most important guest you have ever had in your home for dinner? Well, just imagine what a stir was caused when Jesus and His disciples showed up for dinner at the home of Lazarus, Mary, and Martha (Luke 10:38-42). Martha went immediately into high gear and tore into preparing food for her VIP guests. At some point Martha became frustrated. Without thinking, she complained to Jesus because Mary, her sister and helper, was sitting at His feet listening to Him while He taught instead of assisting with the serving.

Sure, preparations for dinner needed to be made. And 12 guests for dinner is a houseful! But this is how Jesus evaluated Mary's choice to stop her busy serving, sit at His feet, and listen to Him: "Mary has chosen that good part, which will not be taken away from her" (verse 42). It's sort of like Jesus was saying, "Listen, Martha, you have all your life to fix and serve food, but today you have Me. Don't berate your sister. Mary made a most excellent choice." (And I know it's not in the Bible passage, but I like to imagine that perhaps Jesus moved slightly to one side and made a place for Martha to sit down right next to Him.)

It's Your Choice

I'm sure you already know your actions are a matter of choice. You also know that some choices are made for you because they are out of your control. You have no control over things like your work hours, the city or school bus schedules, the times for your church services.

You get the picture.

But multitudes of choices arrive with each new day—almost at the rate of one per minute!—which are yours to make. And these choices, my friend, are a matter of your will. You get to decide what you will or won't do, how you will or won't act. You get to make the choices, which means you can't blame anyone else for what happens next! Hopefully if you are not already making good, better, and best choices, our time together will help you learn to choose wisely.

Just one more thing as we begin: You cannot take back a wrong choice or any of its undesired consequences. But you can *choose* to *learn* from each wrong choice. You can *log* those wrong choices and purpose to *leave* them behind. With the experience behind you, and with God's help, you will do better the next time. You will make a better choice!

But regardless, our wonderful God wants to step in and help you take the shattered pieces of your life and put them back together with the salvation and grace that comes from accepting Jesus as Savior and walking by His Spirit. Nothing that has happened in your life is beyond the loving hands of the God of all comfort, the God of all grace, the God of all healing, and especially the God who loves you unconditionally regardless of your past—and regardless of your poor choices! What a great God you have and serve!

God's Guidelines for Making Right Choices

The following guidelines will help you proceed through your day, confident that you are seeking to make the right choices.

~ *Treat each day as being important.* "Teach us to number our days, that we may gain a heart of wisdom" (Psalm 90:12).

~ *Acknowledge your need for wisdom—and ask for it!* "If any of you lacks wisdom, let him ask of God, who gives to all liberally and without reproach, and it will be given to him" (James 1:5).

~ *Develop a deep respect for God.* "The fear of the LORD is the beginning of wisdom, and the knowledge of the Holy One is understanding" (Proverbs 9:10).

~ *Maintain a vital relationship with Jesus.* "…that the God of our Lord Jesus Christ, the Father of glory, may give to you the spirit of wisdom and revelation in the knowledge of Him" (Ephesians 1:17).

~ *Pay any price for the truth.* "Buy the truth, and do not sell it, also wisdom and instruction and understanding" (Proverbs 23:23).

2

Seven Steps for Making Right Choices

The wise woman builds her house,
but the foolish pulls it down with her own hands.
—Proverbs 14:1

Oh, the life of a writer! You approach a book one way… only to discover about halfway through getting it on paper, there's a really serious change you've got to make!

That's exactly what happened to me in the course of writing this book. Initially, my big plan was to close this book on *A Woman's Guide to Making Right Choices* with a chapter entitled "Seven Steps of Wisdom." These are seven actions that have helped me as I seek to make right choices. But as I was clicking away on my computer's keyboard knowingly postponing the sharing of this incredible, life-changing, life-saving list, I realized I had made a wrong decision—or in keeping with the title of this book, a wrong *choice*. I had a right choice to make, and that choice was a decision to put these Seven Steps of Wisdom right up front. You see, these seven actions make up a short list— possibly even a shortcut—to making right choices.

I also know (from personal experience!) that not everyone finishes a book, or reads through the final chapter. So I decided—or, I made the choice—to share this list right up front. And it comes to you here and now with a prayer that, beginning today, with the very next choice or decision you must make, you'll put this list to work for you.

Where did this list come from? I created it during my first decade as a Christian as I studied, over and over again, through my wonderful Bible—the book that holds all the answers to all our questions and all our problems. The book that contains God's wisdom regarding all the instructions and information we need for making decisions and right choices. These seven components from Scripture aim us toward achieving (or at least getting closer to) wisdom. Put another way, they lead us and assist us in making right choices.

Help for Your Journey Through Life

From experience, I can promise you these Seven Steps of Wisdom will help you with the choices of your life. They have helped me be a helpful and solid wife to my Jim while he transitioned through his careers as a pharmacist, a corporate employee, a seminary student, a pastor and seminary professor, and a missionary, as well as an author and speaker, and currently as he is serving as an associate pastor at the church where we are members.

These principles have also assisted me in raising two daughters. As a mom of two girls only 13 months apart in age, each minute of each day brought a challenge—or 50! And there I was, remembering to follow these steps of wisdom. Today my girls are married to busy, responsible husbands, dads, and providers, and the moms of eight children between them.

These steps of wisdom have also guided me in being God's kind of daughter to my parents while super busy at home with my own family, all the way through to tending to them as aging and ailing parents in their final years and days.

Like you, I've had to make tough decisions and hard choices about daily life issues—and still do. The vast scope of incidents I've faced include just about any and every size of trial, emergency, surprise, and tragedy. And these seven steps have aided me every step of the way—choice by choice—down through the years.

So, are you ready? If so, here we go!

Seven Steps of Wisdom

Step 1: Stop!

Picture this. You are merrily going through your day. So far, so good. For a patch of time, it's been smooth waters. Maybe you're thinking, *Wow, look at me go! See me sail! There's not even been a speed bump. Life is sweet!*

And then…everything goes sideways. The phone rings. The mail arrives. A neighbor drops by. An accident occurs. Your boss goes ballistic. The kids get home from school, or your husband from work. And everything—all that peace and order and well-being and control that had you soaring through your perfect day—falls apart. It's like out of nowhere someone shot a torpedo into your beautiful little boat. You're shocked, or hurt, or blindsided, or utterly surprised, or blown away. The proverbial rug is pulled out from under you.

What is the general first response most people make when something like this occurs? In a word, *reaction*. Your natural tendency is to strike back, talk back, react, blow up, fall apart, cry, throw your hands in the air and give up. Your pride is wounded.

Maybe you are even physically hurt. Or your feelings are injured. You're confused.

Well, right here, at this very juncture, your first choice has got to be to stop. I think of it as coming to a screeeeeching halt! Just put the brakes on—on your emotions, on your mouth, on your actions. Just *stop!* And might I say, *stop quickly!*

Why? Because the surest way to make a wrong choice is to rush before reasoning. To fail to stop and think before acting. To make a quick or snap or emotional decision without making sure you know the right way to handle a situation, or before you know the right decision to make.

You can see it right in your Bible: "He sins who *hastens* with his feet" (Proverbs 19:2). You can also read that "the mouth of the wicked pours forth evil" while "the heart of the righteous studies how to answer," and "the heart of the wise teaches his mouth, and adds learning to his lips" (Proverbs 15:28; 16:23).

If you *stop* before you speak, you live out one of my favorites: "Even a fool is counted wise when he holds his peace; when he shuts his lips, he is considered perceptive" (Proverbs 17:28). Put another way, better to stop and keep your mouth shut and be thought of as a woman of wisdom and understanding, than to open it and prove you are a fool. Once again, just *stop.*

Failure can happen oh so quickly! It's like lightning. One minute all is well, and the next brings the crash and the devastation. All you have to do is fail to stop before you do anything, fail to stop before you act, fail to stop before you move, fail to stop before you speak, and you're probably off the right path. You've failed.

Sure, there are some decisions that have to be made instantaneously. But even if your house is on fire, or there's a terrible accident or medical emergency, or the baby's on the way *now*, you can still stop even for a millisecond and take a breath, and blitz through some options, and shoot up a "Help, Lord!" That one or two split-second stop can help you form a plan on the go while zooming onward to handle a crisis.

So stop. That's Step 1. *Then* you can begin to look and listen. Then you can look for help. Then you can look for solutions. Then you can look for answers. And then you can listen to the wise counsel of others, and most of all, to the still, small voice of God guiding and instructing you about how to handle your problem His way.

Step 2: Wait

Stopping and waiting can merge together because they flow so naturally into each other. Once you stop before doing *anything,* you buy yourself time to start the process of deciding to do *something...* or maybe even *nothing.* Waiting before acting or reacting also buys you time to make a real decision.

I know many times waiting has given me the opportunity to make the decision and choice to do nothing. Other times, waiting has given me time to think a thing through. When someone says something hurtful and personal to me, if I stop and do nothing, then I won't strike back. I won't tell him or her off. I won't preach or lecture. And the end result is that I won't mess up. I won't goof. I won't get tripped up in my emotions and fall into sin.

If I can just wait out a situation, it will buy me time to later— maybe in the car, or once I'm home or have distanced myself from the situation—think about what might have caused this woman to say this destructive or painful thing to me. Sometimes love supplies the reason for someone's behavior. Other times love has to go and talk things over, even confront the other person.

I have to tell you that many times, because I've waited to act or respond, I have been able to give someone the benefit of the doubt. For instance, maybe I know the woman who lashed out has a hard situation at home, and I need to remember to pray for her. Other times, waiting has given me time to remember I am not responsible for another person's behavior, but I am fully responsible for mine!

And waiting gives you control. Ever heard of counting to ten? Well, it helps! It purchases you time to look to God and tap into His fruit of the Spirit "self-control"—along with lots of God's "love, joy, peace, longsuffering, kindness, goodness, faithfulness, [and] gentleness" (Galatians 5:22-23).

Waiting also gives you time to put on "the incorruptible beauty of a gentle and quiet spirit, which is very precious in the sight of God" (1 Peter 3:4). *Gentle* means that you do not provoke others, while *quiet* means you do not respond to the disturbances caused by others.

Waiting gives you the time you need to be the woman of wisdom who "studies *how* to answer" and *what* to say (Proverbs 15:28).

Waiting gives you time to take a deep breath—both in your lungs and in your soul—so you can respond like the woman in Proverbs 31 did: "She opens her mouth with wisdom, and on her tongue is the law of kindness" (verse 26).

I like this quip (which was not meant to be a quip) that points to the value of waiting before reacting: "Always put off until tomorrow that which you shouldn't do at all."[4] In other words, waiting and postponing wrong choices, wrong actions, and reactions can keep you from doing something you absolutely should not do—ever!

Are you wondering how long do you wait? Again, if the house is on fire, don't wait too long! (I keep mentioning the house on fire because my husband and I have had that experience!) If you need to dial 9-1-1, *while* you're reaching for your cell phone or on your way to picking up the house phone, pause mentally, think about the situation, determine what your first action *should* be, think about God and His presence and care for you, and wait on the Lord—for His calm and His direction.

I can also tell you that in some instances I have waited a

day, or a week, or a month, or even up to a year or more before I knew the right way to proceed or the right way to handle a tough situation. You may have times when you also need to wait a while too. And while you are waiting and because you waited, you have time to spend in God's Word, hearing what He has to say to you. And you have sweet, precious time to wait on God in prayer as you talk your situation over with Him.

Step 3: Search the Scriptures

To paraphrase Socrates, "The wisest man is the one who knows his own ignorance." So let's start right there—with our ignorance. I don't know how many times you've read through the Bible, or how many Bible classes you've attended or Bible courses you've completed. However, when you have an issue, or a problem or predicament, you still need to approach the Scriptures themselves in a fresh way to find out what God says about it.

So until you have looked to God first, resist the temptation to rush to your best friend or a sister, or to get on the phone with your mom. What you need is God's input and His perspective and direction—not your girlfriends' opinions, commiseration, or someone you can count on to side with you because she is a close, emotional, or familial connection. You are not looking for sympathy. You are not looking for a "yes friend." You are not looking for someone who will take your side regardless. You are not looking for comfort. And you're certainly not looking for someone else's *reaction*.

What you *are* looking for and need is God's clear, unvarnished, straightforward, perfect, and *right* advice, because your goal is to make the *right* choice. As the psalmist described God's Word, he wrote, "The law of the LORD is perfect...sure...[and] right" (Psalm 19:7-8). You can't go wrong when you search the Scriptures.

Of course, in a tragedy you'll want your family and friends to know right away what's happened. And you'll definitely want— and need—their prayers, and most probably their presence and help. But for the everyday challenging (Uh oh! My child needs to be disciplined…again!) or puzzling (What was that all about?) or painful incidents (What in the world caused her to say that to me, or about me?) that you must handle, go to God. Go to His Word. And the sooner, the better!

Step 4: Pray

First thing, stop. Check!

Next, wait. It's hard, but okay, check!

Next, search the Scriptures. Check! And you're probably feeling better already.

And now, it's time to pray.

(Exhale. Whew!) Whatever happened that sent you down this path of Seven Steps to Wisdom was most likely jarring, confusing, painful…or all of the above. And the steps you've been taking are steps that have moved you to a more peaceful place in your mind and spirit. You can't help but calm down after you've stopped, waited, and spent time in God's Word. All of these *actions* have led you to inactivity, to quietness, and to repose. They have helped settle your emotions; they have neutralized your feelings.

And the choice to go before God in prayer leads you to follow God's command to "be still, and know that I am God" (Psalm 46:10). Or, as several other versions of this verse put it, "Stop your striving," and "Pause a while."[5]

In other words, God calls you to stop all your warlike activity—your fretting and stewing and struggling and your angry reactions—and let things be. It's time to tear your focus away from yourself and your problems and turn it upward to God.

When you need wisdom and direction, pray. Seek God with a humble, open, searching heart—a heart that *knows* it needs help, a heart that *desires* help, a heart that trusts God and is willing to *obey* His instructions.

Whenever a crisis inserts itself into your day—and it will!—and your day begins to unravel, you have some decisions to make. You have to handle it—the crisis, the decision, the confrontation, the emergency. I've discovered a set of questions that I ask myself (usually in a prayer to God). As I send my cry for help up to Him, answers begin to emerge that clear the dark waters and point me to a solution. They begin to reveal the choice that's best.

Why would I do this (whatever is being asked or demanded of me)?

Why would I not do this?

Why should I do this?

Why should I not do this?

The first two questions will bring my motives—both good and bad—to the surface. And the second two questions will reveal my convictions based on the Bible. I know this may sound simplistic. And I know it may seem hazy or look like there's no way this exercise would help. All I can say is it does!

For example, let's say you are moving through your well-planned day. Your phone rings and it's a friend asking, "Hey, want to meet me for lunch?" or "Want to round up the kids and meet at the pool?" What do you do? Quickly run through these questions. Maybe the answer will come on the spot as you think through these questions. Or maybe you'll need to call your friend back in five minutes…or fifteen minutes…or in an hour.

I also have a final end-all question: "Lord, what is the right thing to do?"

Ideally, your aim is to be in constant communion with God

in your mind and heart at all times as you progress through the minutes—and challenges—of your days. As one of my pastors continually reminded his congregation, "Every breath God allows you to breathe in should be exhaled in a prayer." Then, when the crisis occurs, you are already tuned in to God and can immediately start talking your situation over with Him, asking Him for His guidance.

Sounds great, doesn't it? As I said, this is the ideal. But the opposite is usually the case. I know this because I'm a person who slips up in my walk with God and gets selfish, careless, and distracted. I get my eyes off God and forget to stay in constant touch. I forget my walk with Him. Or I turn away from the path of doing things His way. And then, when the crisis occurs—and again, it *will*—and my day begins to unravel, I'm caught off guard and out of touch with the Lord.

The solution? Get things right with God ASAP! Confess sin. Acknowledge Him. Turn away from your less-than-perfect thoughts and behavior and attitudes, and get back in sync with God. Then, *then*, you can begin to interact with Him through prayer, whether you're racing forward in a life-or-death crisis (you know, the house is on fire!) or if you can actually stop and sit, bow, or kneel before your Father who is in heaven and pray. As the quote goes regarding crisis, "If you are swept off your feet, it's time to get on your knees."[6]

Step 5: Seek Counsel

Second-century Roman playwright Plautus accurately observed, "No man is wise enough by himself." Or as the Bible observes, "The way of a fool is right in his own eyes" (Proverbs 12:15). And that is why you and I need this next crucial step for helping us make right choices—seek counsel. Of course, before

Plautus stated this truth, God had already said it many times. In the book of Proverbs we read, "Without counsel, plans go awry, but in the multitude of counselors they are established." And, "Where there is no counsel, the people fall; but in the multitude of counselors there is safety." And, "Plans are established by counsel; by wise counsel wage war" (Proverbs 15:22; 11:14; 20:18).

I have been so blessed to have been surrounded by many truly biblical older women, the kind described in Titus 2:3-5. And believe me, through my correspondence and ministry to women around the world, I know this is rare! My most-often-asked question is, "I want to grow, and I know I need help, but where are the older women?" I thank God for the seasoned women in my church who followed God's mandate and made themselves available to me and to other women in the church who craved advice, counsel, encouragement, even a friend committed to praying for them.

And, in time, as I grew and matured, I dedicated my ministry to teaching the Bible to women in a way that changes their lives. In time it was my turn to pass on what I had learned. And these seven steps are one of those invaluable lessons.

Step 6: Make a Decision

So, let's backtrack and review: You have a problem or an issue you are facing. Hopefully you've stopped. No blurts or blunders so far. No screaming or yelling (unless the house is on fire). No one's been hurt verbally or physically by you...all because you stopped.

Then, also hopefully, you waited. Maybe you needed to cool down emotionally, and you did. Maybe you needed to take deep breaths physically, maybe even take a step back physically from the situation. Maybe you even went to your room or withdrew from your trying situation, as I've done many a time to collect myself and my thoughts about what was happening or needed to be done.

And as you waited, you bought time for yourself to search the Scriptures, to seek the counsel and the mind of the Lord. It comforts me to know that, as the Bible says, "there is nothing new under the sun" (Ecclesiastes 1:9). That means what I'm looking at has been faced before, by countless millions! That what I'm suffering has been suffered before, by countless other women, wives, moms, daughters, employees, neighbors, and on and on goes the list.

God's job is to give counsel to you (and He's done His job perfectly and thoroughly). All you have to do is search for it and find it! That's your job.

And you've prayed. I can't even think of prayer or say the word without exhaling—whew! Prayer is the letdown of emotions and tension. It's the physical unwind. It's the pushing aside of all that is worldly and bothersome and centering on one thing and one thing only—your heavenly Father. I love these first four steps because they are quiet steps. Calm steps. And they are done alone. They physically quiet your heart and mind and body. They position you. After taking these steps, your decision will be one based on wisdom, not emotion. Then you can verify your choice or decision with the wisdom of wise counselors. They are to be a sounding board for you as you make your decision. They may help, but ultimately it's your decision, your choice to act upon!

Step 7: Act on Your Decision

Now it's time for action. (This doesn't mean you won't or shouldn't make corrections or alterations along the way as you go.) To launch your decision, have a plan. What will you say?

How will you act? What will your first step be? Do you need to rehearse? Like a general marching into war, move out and move forward on your plan. *General* Dwight D. Eisenhower, who became *President* Dwight D. Eisenhower, ran the US Army and the United States of America with a motto: "Planning is everything."[7] Form a good plan (that encompasses Steps 1-6). Then, by faith, execute it (Step 7). Be bold. Be confident. Why? Because you've done the work. You've moved, decently and in order, toward a solution to a problem or a difficult or potentially life-changing decision.

It's Your Choice

My friend, I cannot begin to tell you how much these seven steps have meant in my life! As you know all too well, each and every day is filled to overflowing with issues to conquer, challenges to face, problems to solve, people to handle, and time to manage. You have probably been thinking throughout this chapter, *I don't have time to stop and go through all these steps! I've got a family, a career, a ministry, and a life that needs to be lived!* But, my friend, you *can't* afford not to take these steps. For without these steps or something like them, you will end up making wrong choices, which will mean more time backtracking, starting over, spinning your wheels, apologizing, mopping up messes, and wallowing in sorrow and regret. I know from experience. So, rethink your outlook. Make some changes—some choices! With just a few precious moments of prayerful consideration, you can make better choices.

What will it be?

It's your choice!

God's Guidelines for Making Right Choices

These guidelines will help you proceed through your day, confident that you are seeking to make the right choices.

~ *Always choose to do what's right*—"to him who knows to do good and does not do it, to him it is sin" (James 4:7).

~ *Consult your Bible before making decisions*—"Your word is a lamp to my feet and a light to my path" (Psalm 119:105).

~ *Make no decision without prayer*—"Be anxious for nothing, but in everything by prayer and supplication, with thanksgiving, let your requests be made known to God" (Philippians 4:6).

~ *Seek counsel before making decisions*—"Without counsel, plans go awry, but in the multitude of counselors they are established" (Proverbs 15:22).

~ *Believe God has your best in mind*—"If you then, being evil, know how to give good gifts to your children, how much more will your Father who is in heaven give good things to those who ask Him" (Matthew 7:11).

3

Getting a Jump on Your Day

This is the day the LORD has made;
we will rejoice and be glad in it.
—PSALM 118:24

Are you looking for help on how to make every day a great day? Well, here is the "can't miss first choice"—getting up! And I've already made it. This is the toughest "right choice" a woman has to make first thing each and every day of her life. And I made it—I got up. (And I didn't even hit the snooze button a time or two).

Maybe you're thinking, *What's the big deal about that? Everyone eventually wakes up. And everyone gets up sooner or later in the day.*

That's true. And it's those rare mornings that we can afford to sleep in that we girls long for and love. But the truth? Lazy days of sleeping in until you wake up is a treat we rarely get to enjoy—such as when we're on vacation, or it's our birthday. And that is doubly true if you have small children and a bustling household!

But what about our workdays? Our day-in, day-out days? You know, the real-life days when every minute matters and each

60-second time interval is vitally important? When others are counting on you, whether at home or at work, or both?

As stellar as getting up this morning was, it wasn't easy. In fact, it hurt. Bad. Really bad. (Did I mention today is a Monday?!)

A Reality Check

But just about every morning, at the sound of that dreaded alarm-clock buzz tone, I get up—especially if I recall some stone-cold facts and convincing reasons for rising and attempting to shine.

First, I have a plan. This helps me remember, somewhere in the dullness of identifying what that horrible noise is, that, the night before, prior to putting my head on my pillow, I made a plan for my fresh new day—a plan that will work only if I get up when I planned to get up. There is nothing more practical than a plan.

Then I have a motive. I know in my heart that my plan was made because of a motive, a passionate desire for something I think is significant, and a dream or two of some accomplishment that will benefit others or fulfill a personal goal. There is nothing more powerful than a motive.

Next, I have a need. I hate this, but I have to acknowledge that there must be a bona fide need to get up, or it may not happen! Others need me and are depending on me. For food—on the breakfast table, in their backpacks and briefcase. For transportation—to and from school or work or a bus stop. For an appointment—whether it's the dentist or a radio interview. For clean clothes. For groceries in the cupboard. On and on goes my List of Things I Need to Do to take care of myself, my work, and others. It's longer than a child's list for Christmas gifts! For me, my personal workplace is at home—which may or may not be better than going out of the house to a job site. But I need to be at my desk at a certain time so I can do certain tasks, take care of vital communication, and, of course, write. There's nothing more persuasive than a need.

Oh, and then I have a schedule. When I'm tempted to lie in bed murmuring, *Just a few more minutes won't hurt*, that's when my schedule starts rolling through my semi-consciousness. And that starts shaking me awake as my mind switches gears to thinking, *If I don't get up now, I won't get my power walk today...and I won't get my before-breakfast projects and work taken care of... which will throw me behind for the rest of the day*. And I know from experience that if that happens, I'll get frustrated and be anxious all day long because I'm running behind. I'll never be able to get that hour or half-hour back. Having a workable, fine-tuned schedule in mind is a powerful nudge that rolls me out from under the covers. There's nothing more propelling than a schedule.

And finally, lots of will. Willpower is revealed every time you make a conscious choice. And this book is all about the choices you—and I—make. As the saying goes, "Where there's a will, there's a way." There's nothing more productive than willpower.

Whew! All of this...just to get out of bed in the morning. But this one first and primary daily right choice requires a plan, a motive or dream or desire, a purpose, a need, a schedule, and loads of will. Then, once you're up, you begin to live out one of my favorite sayings, "Life begins when you get moving."[8]

Looking for a Better Life

Just last week I completed another quarterly taping session of my radio broadcast *A Woman After God's Own Heart*. As I was rehearsing the content of the programming, I noted that one of my spot features began with this lead-in: "I hear these words so often from Christian women—I feel rushed and spent! I can only wonder, what are we doing to ourselves?"

It doesn't matter what country or what language women's heart-cries emerge from, busyness is a mammoth problem. And, as you know all too well, whenever we go looking for the solution to our Number One problem of busyness, we always work our way back to a flaw in the way we manage our time. If we ever get fed up enough to say, "That's it! I'm not going to live this way anymore!" and analyze what it is we are trying to do with our time, want to do with our time, and need to do with our time, our investigation will lead us back through the evidence and clues that clearly uncover the poor choices we are making regarding the time God has given us.

The problem? Plain and simple, it's poor time management. And the solution? Also plain and simple—better time management.

To make better choices and work toward a better life, we need to realize we are making poor choices about how we spend our time for one of two reasons: We either know how to manage our time and are choosing not to, or we need help with time management. We need to know the time-proven principles for time and life management.

Finding Help

Maybe because I failed so miserably in my homemaking (I mean, how was I to know that you wash beans before you cook them so you rinse out the grit and rocks?) and time management roles as a young wife and mom for the first eight years of my marriage, I still look for a better life. Which means I am always searching for time management tips. And because you're reading this book, I'm sure you're interested in finding help as well.

When my husband enrolled in seminary, a golden opportunity appeared for me. The college and seminary library was
vast! Realizing this free resource was a gift from God, Jim and I
arranged our schedules so I could go with him to the seminary
campus one day a week while our girls were at school. There I
could luxuriate for several hours in the library's stacks and carrels
while he attended classes.

Guess where I spent these precious hours? In the practical
sections of the library. In the business section. In the management section. In the self-help section. And did my "self" ever
need help!

There, in that library, I stumbled on wonderful treasures.
I went crazy! I pulled book after book down off those loaded
shelves. Time management books? I'll take them all. How-to-
get-your-act-together books? I'll take them too!

At that stage of my marriage and family life, I was hardly
able to hold my head above water. I had a hyperactive family of
four going at full speed in the fast lane in every direction at once.
I was the wife of a busy associate pastor who was also working
on a master's degree in theology. I was trying to take care of my
home as well as open its doors and our hearts in hospitality. I
was committed to meeting my family's needs while also trying
to serve in my church in some area of ministry. But, "How, oh
how?" I asked God.

I craved help for a better life. And I had already taken the
first giant step toward improvement and growth: I had identified,
named, labeled, and owned my key problem—my life was a mess.

Along with that admission came a refusal to rationalize and
excuse my messed-up ways with trite excuses like, "But you
don't understand. We're a v-e-r-y busy family! One of these days,
things will ease up and then I'll have more time to take care of
my home and family…er, and myself."

Yes, I identified the problem—my problem. That was Step 1. And by visiting a library and reading advice and wisdom from experts on time management, I was tackling Step 2—I was taking action to do something about my defect. I was choosing to move toward a better life that brought some peace and order out of chaos.

Oh yes, I was definitely looking for that better life. I got tired of thinking—and even blurting out once in a while—*There has got to be more to life than this!* Meaning there's got to be more to life than all my wheel-spinning, than my feeling rushed and spent all the time and still not getting my life in order. Instead, I was confused and out of control.

As I am writing about this memory, recalling those trips in the car with my husband to his seminary library (which was better—and cheaper!—than any vacation we could afford at that time), I can almost smell the distinct fragrance of the bound books lining wall after wall and aisle after aisle of that quiet building that became an oasis to me. I was the proverbial kid in a candy shop, wondering, *Where should I start? What should I pick first? And how can I have it all?*

Well, whenever I found an especially helpful and simple (I was in the remedial stage!) book on time management, I had Jim check it out of the library for me with his student ID. Then, for one whole week, I pored over that book and typed out notes to go over and over in the hopes of improving my hectic existence. I knew God wanted me to "study to be quiet," to "lead a quiet and peaceable life," to do all things "decently and in order," to diligently "plan my work," and "look well to the ways of [my] household." I just didn't know how.[9]

"But how, oh how?" I kept asking God.

Coming Face-to-Face with Choice #1

Well, praise God, those books came to my rescue! And here is the biggest "how" I got out of them: Almost every single book stressed that the first most important step toward success of any kind is getting up when you need to. I'm sure you agree this is one really simple, but really hard, choice you've got to make—and *can* make—every day. In fact, it's the first choice you must make every day, whether you like it or not. Will you get up when you need to...or not?

It's a choice.

Each morning, when your sleep is shattered by your clock radio or cell phone alarm or buzz, realize that it's right then and right there that you make what could be the most important choice you'll make all day.

It goes like this. If you get up, you are in control of yourself and your day. (Well, at least you're in control of how it begins! After all, you have to leave room for God's plan, for interruptions, even crises.) Why can I say this? Because when you get up, from Minute #1, you are calling the shots. You are in the driver's seat of your day, so to speak. You are working out your plan. You are looking well to the flow of your household and your day.

As you work your way through this book about your life and your choices, you'll see this one singular choice directing the rest of each day. You'll see how Choice #1 affects Choice #2...and #3...and #4...and all the rest of your choices during the day. Imagine a long line of dominoes standing on end. When you push the first domino, it falls into the next... and very quickly, all the rest of the dominoes fall in rapid succession. This, of course, is known as "the domino effect."

I hate to say it, but when you don't get out of your bed on time so you can get things done "decently and in order" (1 Corinthians 14:40)—in a proper and orderly way—the domino effect goes into action and *every*thing suffers for the rest of the day. It's amazing—and frightening!—how that one seemingly small first choice can influence everything else for the next 24 hours.

Big Results Begin with Small Steps

I like to do things in small steps. It's easier that way, and makes success and change more achievable. And, it's also an invaluable time-management principle. So, instead of declaring, "I'm going to get up on time or early every day for the rest of my life," I simply try to get up on time for just one day. That's what I tell myself—it's just one day. I can do this for just one day.

And how important is just one day? Here's a sobering thought: What you are today is what you have been becoming. And what you are today is what you will be in the future...if nothing changes. Every act repeated—either good or bad—is creating the real you and shaping your real life.

Each of your choices—whether good or bad or mediocre—made over and over again becomes a habit. And your goal, and mine too, is to make right choices over and over again until we've established good habits, godly habits.

And what about your dreams? What you want to be and become? What you want to do with your life? What kind of person you want to become? What changes you would like to make in yourself? And in the world? What you want to leave behind?

Well, as ranchers, cattlemen, and farmers said in the Wild, Wild West whenever they needed to get moving—or keep moving—"Daylight is burnin'," which translates into "Let's get to work and get the work done while it's day."

When you get up at the optimal time for accomplishing God's will and your plans, you have the opportunity to make your dreams come true. You get to tackle becoming the unique person God created you to be, and to do the magnificent things He's planned for you—to become a masterpiece, an exquisite work of art. You have all day—16 or more waking hours—to make right choices that move you in the direction of something thrilling, something excellent, something outstanding, something you can be Christian-proud of at the end of the day.

And when you don't get up on time, what happens? Well, you know the answer all too well! You miss opportunities to move toward your goals, to make your dreams happen, or to make someone's life better and easier for them today. As I shared in one of my books for young adult girls, *A Young Woman's Guide to Making Right Choices,* "Oversleeping will never make dreams come true."[10] It's obvious that getting up on time is the first right choice you get to make every day. It's a mega-choice!

A Call to Action

The book of Proverbs is a keen study of opposites. And in Proverbs, the opposite of a woman who gets up and gets going each daybreak is a "sluggard." This word is used to describe someone who has a bad habit of being lazy, slow, or idle. A sluggard is a person who hates to get up and hates to work, and will take forever to get going. If you've ever seen a slug on a sidewalk or driveway, then you get the picture! Here are just a couple gems from Proverbs to motivate you to "get up and at 'em." (That's an expression my parents used to say every day to get me and my three brothers out of bed for school.)

> As a door turns on its hinges, so a sluggard turns on his bed (Proverbs 26:14 NIV).

The next time your alarm goes off and you turn over, remember this proverb!

> How long will you slumber, O sluggard? When will you rise from your sleep? A little sleep, a little slumber, a little folding of the hands to sleep—so shall your poverty come on you like a prowler (Proverbs 6:9-11).

This set of verses asks convicting questions—and then gives you a picture of the result of too much sleep and too little work.

Photo of a "Sluggard"

1. A sluggard will not begin things.
2. A sluggard will not finish things.
3. A sluggard will not face things.[11]

Running with the Giants

I have a passion for learning from the men and women in the Bible. And I try to read everything I can get my hands on that gives me further insights into their faith and trust in God. *Running with the Giants*[12] is the title of a book that highlights a handful of the great giants of the faith in Scripture. As you go through the following, notice the important message each of these "giants" is sending your way.

Jesus—God's Son and our Savior got up early. What did He do once He was awake? "Now in the morning, having risen a long while before daylight, He went out and departed to a solitary place; and there He prayed" (Mark 1:35).

Jesus talked to His heavenly Father first thing in the morning—a long while before daylight! Alone and in the dark, He prayed to God. He received daily strength and direction for doing God's will for one more day—for the day in front of Him. He came away from this first-thing encounter with God armed for facing and handling all kinds of temptation, especially the temptation to turn away from going to the cross.

The Proverbs 31 woman—She is a picture of God's ideal woman. Proverbs 31:10-31 is a Hebrew poem, and each verse highlights one or two of this woman's character qualities. Note what quality is found in verse 15: "She also rises while it is yet night, and provides food for her household, and a portion for her maidservants."

This lady was a super-busy wife and mom and home manager. If she was like you and me, she yearned for each and every day to be better than the day before. To be more organized. To have fewer slip-ups. To be better prepared for her day, whether that day included disciplining a two-year-old whose new favorite word is "No!" or dealing with a depressed husband, whether that day involved managing responsibilities at work (on top of those at home) or making another daily visit to a parent or grandparent in a nursing home.

For her to fulfill one of God's priorities for her—to take care of her family—she had to set her "alarm" and get up and get going early. To her, living life God's way was important enough to make the choice to get a jump start on the day. And, I repeat, she is God's picture of the ideal woman. She sets the pattern for us.

The women at the tomb—Oh, wow! What an example this group of ladies is—how they loved Jesus! When He died on the cross, they were right there to the very end. Then they followed those who carried their friend and Savior's body to see where He was buried. And once they got home, instead of collapsing, they went into high gear and tackled the work of preparing spices for Jesus' body so He could be properly buried. And then "very early in the morning, they…came to the tomb bringing the spices which they had prepared" (Luke 24:1).

Do you think these women were tired? Do you think it was stressing and horrible enough to watch Jesus suffer brutality and die in agony on a cross? And yet they pressed on with their mission—to tend to Jesus' body and burial. What if they had turned on their hinges on their beds like a sluggard on that all-important morning when they needed to minister to the Lord? What if they had made excuses? What if they had slept in?

It All Begins with a Single Step

The saying, "A journey of a thousand miles begins with a single step" says it all, doesn't it? Your dreams and responsibilities are what make up your life's journey. So, to begin your journey of following and fulfilling your dreams and taking care of your responsibilities, you must begin with one single step—get up tomorrow.

What do you want *to do tomorrow?* This question has to do with your goals and dreams. In my case I want to start writing another chapter for this book, and I want to purchase a birthday gift for a special friend. A young college friend of mine wants to give herself a trip to the Holy Land as a graduation gift. And tomorrow? She wants to start an Internet search for tour packages, a key step toward making her dream come true. And a grandmother I know dreams of hosting a family reunion…and tries to work on it every tomorrow until her goal is made real!

To want something means to desire it strongly. What do you strongly desire to achieve tomorrow? Name it. Then write it here in the margin. And on your planner page or cell phone sticky note for tomorrow's date. Then repeat the name-that-goal process at the end of each day, and make it a habit. Knowing what you want to do tomorrow to make progress and take steps toward your dreams is a surefire way to get out of bed tomorrow! In fact, you may be so excited you'll wake up before that awful alarm noise! You won't be dragging yourself out of the rack. No, you'll be springing out, eager to get going on your day and its dream projects.

What do you have *to do tomorrow? Wanting* to do something and *having* to do something are two entirely different things. *Wanting* to do something lies in the realm of dreams and desires. And *having* to do something has to do with taking care of your responsibilities. These are your roles. They encompass your obligations and duties.

So now it's list-making time. Choose to make a list each night of Things I Have to Do Tomorrow. I've even heard it called a Do-or-Die List. Some of the projects that should appear here are givens. These include your responsibilities as a wife, mom, home manager, daughter, student, employer, employee. I personally love my home, and love being at home (after all, that's where I work!). And I love for my home to be tidy and clean. But some days it's hard to love doing eight more loads of laundry. Yet that's a given, it's something that has to be done. And it really blesses my family!

Next up are those givens that could even be categorized as "thorns in the flesh." You know, the ones you have to do but don't want to do. The ones that are so difficult or unpleasant that you keep putting them off. For me it's often keeping up with or getting caught up on correspondence. I know women who adore shopping, but for me, well, just let me stay home and write! But sure enough, fairly regularly I "have" to go shopping. It has to be done, fitted into an over-full schedule that includes serious deadlines and commitments.

After you've written your lists, it's time to try to put the tasks and projects in a priority order. Ask yourself, "If I could do only one thing tomorrow, what would it be? What must it be?" That, of course, will go at the top of your list. Because it's a challenge sometimes to determine priorities, I make it a habit to pray through this decision-making process. I want and need God's guidance as I make choices regarding my schedule. And here's the good news! If all you are able to accomplish is that one priority item—the top one—in your 24-hour-day, you can count your day a success.

Life—and every minute of it—is a precious gift from God. In addition to the life He's given you, He also has incredible plans and grand purposes for you as well. So, as the book title exhorts, *Don't Waste Your Life*. The author, John Piper, pleads:

> Most people slip by in life without a passion for God, spending their lives on trivial diversions, living for comfort and pleasure...[Don't] get caught up in a life that counts for nothing...Learn to live for Christ, and don't waste your life![13]

Can you imagine anything worse than a life that counts for nothing? I'm sitting here with you in my heart, praying, "Oh no, not you!" And I'm praying it for me too. Each day God gifts you with countless opportunities to live with passion, to make a difference, to contribute to others, and to bring honor and glory to Him. But such a day begins with making a choice: choosing to get out of bed, knowing that God has given you a world to conquer, a life to live—to really live—and important work to do that makes a difference!

You can't miss with this choice.

Things to Do Today to Get a Jump on Your Day

As you pray about living your life God's way and purpose to (by His great grace) make each day count, the following steps will pave the way for a better tomorrow. This exercise will help you follow through on your first step toward a more meaningful life—getting out of bed!

Step 1: Determine when you must get up to make your day go the way you want and need it to go.

Step 2: Get to bed in time to get the rest you need before your getting-up time.

Step 3: Set your alarm—a good loud one, an obnoxious one!

Step 4: Pray. Ask for God's help to get up. Tell Him why it's important that you do. Rehearse your plans, purposes, commitments, and dreams for tomorrow with Him. Go ahead. He cares! After all, if they're good ones, they came from Him (Psalm 37:4-5).

Step 5: Purpose to get up…no matter what. Don't give in to your body. And don't worry about not getting enough sleep. It's only for one morning! Remember the adage: Mind over mattress!

Step 6: Praise God when you hear the alarm. Stand beside the psalmist and cry out with the dawn, "This is the day the LORD has made; we will rejoice and be glad in it" (Psalm 118:24).

4
Fanning the Flame of Your Heart

*Your words were found, and I ate them, and Your word
was to me the joy and rejoicing of my heart.*
—JEREMIAH 15:16

Imagine yourself in this scenario. There you are—yes, that's you—sitting up in your warm, cozy bed oh so early in the morning! Last night you decided how you wanted your tomorrow to go. You did the math and chose a time for getting up that would make your today a better day. You set your alarm. And, sure enough, it sounded out its unique horrendous noise at the appointed time. And, miracle of miracles, you leaned over, pushed the off button (no snoozing for you today!), turned on your lamp, sat up in bed, smiled (I hope), greeted your brand new day positively (I hope again), and you are stretching as you throw the covers back and boldly stick one foot...then the other...out from under your covers. And before you know it, you are standing...and then you take your first steps forward. You're up and you're at 'em!

Hallelujah, you are living out the law of physics that states, "An object at rest tends to remain at rest, and an object in motion tends to remain in motion."

Well, if this scene describes your morning, congratulations! Obviously, your heart responded to the idea of taking charge of your day by determining a time to get up, and you did it! And today is Day 2 of your journey to a new you. Today you are continuing on your makeover to take charge of your life and to make the good, better, and best choices. The right choices. And getting up is an obvious first right choice any and every new day. And it's especially meaningful if you get up at the time you calculated when planning the optimal wake-up call.

A Moment of Reflection

I'm sitting at my desk—writing, of course—and thinking of you! I'm wishing I knew how your spiritual journey has unfolded. How you found out about Jesus and His offer of forgiveness and salvation, of a new life. How you were raised—did you attend church or not, were your parents Christians or not? How God has orchestrated your spiritual growth.

I know your story isn't like mine. As the saying goes, "There are many roads to Jesus, but only one way to God." And that is through His Son, Jesus Christ. Jesus tells us in John 14:6 that "no one comes to the Father except through Me" (John 14:6). Whatever your path has been, and whatever means God used to call you to Himself, I hope you are faithful to thank and praise Him with every living breath He allows you to take!

For me, God opened the doors to my heart at age 28. Once Jim and I found a strong, dynamic church, we purchased our first Bibles as a couple who had already been married for eight years. After floundering and failing—and flailing!—as spouses and the parents of two little ones, we dove into those brand new Bibles. We were just like the psalmist, who declared, "My soul thirsts for God" (Psalm 42:2). Yes, we were living in the California desert, but our souls had been in a desert too—and for too long!

Jim and I just couldn't get enough of God's Word! It fed us. It established us. It fortified us. It mended us. And, for the first time we had guidelines for life, for marriage, and for parenting. We knew we needed help and we drank deeply and often from the living water of the Word. We were such babes! I mean, we didn't know anything about the Bible, not even the ages-old stories of Jesus and the great Bible heroes.

We absolutely loved God's Word and set a goal to read through our stiff and shiny new Bibles in a year. And we hungered so much to understand more about what Christ had done for us that we also added reading through the New Testament several times a year.

I have to say, I can't think of anything that I resisted. That may be because I had a need to know…and I knew it. I had a marriage and family to mend and tend to—the right way. I had issues and behaviors that needed radical help and or removal! And above all, I yearned to follow God with all my heart. I didn't want anything to do with doing spiritual- and God-things halfway, with halfheartedness, lukewarmness, weak attempts, or a "giving it the old college try" approach. No, I needed to know *every*thing! And the sooner, the better.

And miracle of miracles, I could hold "everything" in my hands any time I chose to! It was right there in my Bible. As Peter reported, God's "divine power has given to us *all* things that pertain to life and godliness, through the knowledge of Him who called us by glory and virtue" (2 Peter 1:3). Or, put another way, God has given you everything you need to live for Him—to be a woman after His own heart.

First Things First

Are you with me yet? Are you there—at the place of refusing anything halfhearted when it comes to your quest to know God? (Oh, how I wish you could hear me praying for you!)

So, now what?

Well, now that you're up and greeting your brand new day, you obviously require some waking-up time. You need to transition from a zombie state to a living, breathing, heart-ticking and blood-pumping person who can also think and function! Probably some coffee, tea, or hot chocolate—or a large glass of water—will help you move this process along. And a little walking around will get your energy going.

My motto is "begin small"—just move around doing things that don't require any quick or strenuous movements, any heavy thinking or decision making. During this time you'll want to check your schedule for the day so there are no surprises later—like hearing the trash truck zoom past your house and realizing no one set your trash containers out on the curb.

I hope right now you're remembering Choice #1, the one that starts your day off right. That choice is getting up at the time you must in order to do the things you want to do and have to do.

I can't resist sharing a timely quote from a "Life Is Sweet" 2012 daily desk calendar that I gave as Christmas gifts this year: "The achievement of your goal is assured the moment you commit yourself to it."[14] I'm hoping and believing you have committed yourself to the goal to get up and get going so your days—and life—are sweet!

And now we are on to Choice #2!

Reality Check!

Read your Bible is Choice #2, right?

But wait…! Because you are awake, and because you are starting to think about what's ahead of you today, you are also beginning to remember all the urgent, important, necessary, and even a few fun things that are scheduled for this bright new day. And, if you're not on guard, you will begin to realize that unless you start cutting out some things, you won't get it all done—especially if you take time to read your Bible. So guess what happens next? The great time-managing mistress in you starts lopping things off, usually starting with your Bible time. You may even promise yourself, *I'm sure I'll have some time at lunch, or during a break in my day, or surely there will be some time this evening to read my Bible!*

And guess what? At the end of the day, you still haven't read one word out of God's Word—His personal love letter and instruction book to you! You forgot that "all Scripture is given by inspiration of God, and is profitable" (2 Timothy 3:16).

Now, what can you say about all that other stuff you did during your day? Can you say any of it was "profitable"? I'm sure some of it was—your family, your home, your work and education, and your ministry are, after all, your priorities. But maybe not that side trip by the bakery for a cinnamon roll and coffee? Or that fabulous sale going on at your favorite department store? (Never mind your closet is already stuffed full!)

But by contrast—and without question—you can be perfectly assured that any amount of time you spend reading your Bible is time spent excellently because you are involved in a 100 percent profitable activity. This seems like such a no-brainer, but I'll say it anyway: Start your day in a guaranteed-to-be-profitable way by spending time with God.

I love the perspective on time spent in Bible reading given to us from the heart and words of George Muller. They convict me because, while we so often try to figure out a shortcut when it comes to our time in God's Word, this man shows us the opposite mind-set. Meet him now, and remember him well, for you'll learn more about him in the next chapter...

A Christian evangelist, George Muller was also the director of the now-legendary Ashley Down Orphanage in Bristol, England. It was there that Muller, by faith in the promises of God and fervent prayer, cared for all the needs—food, clothing, health, and education—of 10,024 orphans in his life. His words point us to daily seek out the knowledge of God and the strength available to us in the Bible. Let his words speak to your heart and ignite your passion for God's Word as you face the daily needs you have.

> The vigor of our spiritual life will be in exact proportion to the place held by the Bible in our life and thoughts. I solemnly state this from the experience of fifty-four years. The first three years after conversion I neglected the Word of God. Since I began to search it diligently, the blessing has been wonderful. I have read the Bible through one hundred times, and always with increasing delight. Each time it seems like a new book to me. Great has been the blessing from consecutive, diligent, daily study. I look upon it as a lost day when I have not had a good time over the Word of God.[15]

And moving right along, we come to Choice #2! After getting out of bed, choose to spend time with God. It's now your sacred, precious time to look to God for all the things (attitudes, purpose, commitment, and perspective) you are going to need today.

For instance, strength—who ever has enough of it? And wisdom—your every decision and encounter requires this quality. Joy—sure, you can plaster on a phony smile, and it's hard to have joy when your days are too full, but God is the giver of the fruit of the Spirit, His joy. And discipline—we can make all the to-do lists in the world and painstakingly create a schedule in fine-tuned detail, but it is God who spurs us on to follow through and to keep on keeping on.

Your choice to take time to read the Bible on the front end of your fresh new day is vital. Even with all your planning and preparations, your day is still an unknown—but it is known to God. One thing you can be sure about is that your unknown day will—it will!—include roadblocks, trials, challenges, surprises, heartaches, and a plethora of decisions to be made. Jesus said it Himself: "In the world you will have tribulation" (John 16:33).

But you can just as surely count on God's blessings, His abundant and all-sufficient grace (He promises "My grace is sufficient for you"—2 Corinthians 12:9), and the unmistakable evidence of His love and joy sprinkled over, throughout, and all around the issues of your day.

> So before your day gets going…
> or gets out of hand…
> and before the day's demands begin their assault…
> and before people invade your solitude and space,
> do this one thing: Seek the Lord.

Spend time with your heavenly Father learning from Him through His Word. Once you're up, choose to make God your Number One priority. Choose to put first things first. Choose to meet with Him before the day gets rolling. This step—this one choice—will really set the tone of your day…and your voice… and your words…and your actions…and your attitudes…and the way you treat people, starting right at home under your very own roof.

And yes, I can hear you—as I so often hear myself—thinking, *I just don't have time to stop and spend time with God. It's just not possible today. I mean, I have people to see, places to go, and things to do!*

But oh how wrong we are with this kind of reasoning! This sort of rationale discounts the fact that the Bible is a special book, because it's a spiritual book. In fact, it's the greatest book ever written! And if you are a Christian, God's Spirit—the Holy Spirit—speaks to you as you read God's Word. That's why it's so important to spend time reading it. For when you do, you will think differently. You will live differently. You will grow spiritually. You will handle the practical day-in and day-out matters in your path differently. And you will make choices that have the mark of God and godly wisdom written all over them.

And, oh, how blessed you will be! Don't you think this starter-list of benefits and blessings makes it worth the simple effort of getting up a few minutes early so you can bury yourself, heart and soul, into God's Word—at least for a little while? And what may be the most compelling reason to link up with God each dawn is this startling, challenging statement Jesus made: "without Me you can do nothing" (John 15:5).

Please, don't choose to be a "nothing" woman. Choose instead to be a "something" woman! Read your Bible first thing. Then step out into your fresh new day and bear fruit for Jesus, fruit that benefits the people in your day and brings glory to your God and Savior—fruit, more fruit, and much fruit!

Count Your Blessings

Blessings abound when you turn to God's Word. And what a blessing you receive when you make that second choice! For instance,

The Bible keeps you from wrong behavior—"Your word I have hidden in my heart, that I might not sin against You" (Psalm 119:11). Scripture teaches and instructs you. It rebukes you when and where you are wrong. It points out sin in your life. It corrects you and straightens out your thinking and choices. And it trains and equips you to live for God, helping you choose to do what is right.

The Bible leads you in the right direction—"Your word is a lamp to my feet and a light to my path" (Psalm 119:105). My husband and I take our morning walks early while it is still dark. So we take a flashlight for safety and guidance. But back when Psalm 119 was written, light was provided by a simple lighted wick that was soaking in oil poured into a crude piece of pottery that was held in the palm of a hand. Whether you use a lighted wick, a flashlight, or the face of your cell phone, light in darkness gives you confidence as you move forward. It also keeps you from wandering off the path. And it prevents you from tripping up on an obstacle and suffering an injury.

When it comes to your walk with God, and making right choices so you are following Him with all your heart, God's Word points the way. It gives you the truth you need for making right decisions and moral choices.

The Bible guides you in the truth—"All Scripture is given by inspiration of God, and is profitable for doctrine, for reproof, for correction, for instruction in righteousness" (2 Timothy 3:16).

There are very few things you can be completely sure of. But the Bible is in its own rare, for-sure category. "All Scripture"—all of the Bible, 100 percent of it—is 100 percent from God, 100 percent inspired by Him, 100 percent true, 100 percent pure, and 100 percent helpful and useful. You never have to doubt anything you read in the Bible.

And, can you handle another added blessing? It is "profitable." All—100 percent—of the time you spend in God's Word is 100 percent profitable. It's useful. It's guaranteed to be time well spent.

The Bible prepares you to serve others—"...that the [servant] of God may be complete, thoroughly equipped for every good work" (2 Timothy 3:17). What an incredible result the Word of God has in our lives! My favorite words in this verse are "complete," "thoroughly," and "every." Think about it: God's Word makes you "capable and proficient in everything [you] are called to be or do."[16] It "thoroughly" equips and enables you to live righteously. And this equipping extends to your service in "every" good work.

The Bible sharpens your discernment or judgment—"The word of God is living and powerful...and is a discerner of the thoughts and intents of the heart" (Hebrews 4:12). As you read the Bible, dramatic things happen. Just as you cannot be near a fire without feeling its warmth, you cannot read the Bible and not be affected by it. It is alive! And it is powerful! It is dynamite. It's as if whenever you approach the word of God, the ground is already rumbling. So just go ahead. Pick up your Bible...and prepare yourself to have your world rocked! God's Word will—it will!—change your life. And one of those changes will be in your perspective on life issues. You will be viewing the world and your decisions the way God views them. You will catch yourself thinking about things the way God thinks about them. You will be more sensitive to the way you are choosing to live and the choices you are making as Scripture discerns your thoughts and the motives of your heart.

The Bible gives instructions for eternal life—"From childhood you [Timothy] have known the Holy Scriptures, which are able to make you wise for salvation through faith which is in Christ Jesus" (2 Timothy 2:15). These words were spoken about the man, Timothy, a mighty man of God. Thanks to his godly mom and grandmom, who faithfully taught him God's Word, Timothy heard and knew the truths of the gospel. The path for salvation and eternal life was laid out for him.

Getting into God's Word

Can you see why making the choice to spend time with God in His Word is so important? It kicks off a progression toward spiritual growth and maturity. Getting into the Bible and having a quiet time alone with God causes you to grow—grow in the knowledge of Him, which helps you grow in making better choices, which causes you to grow in Christlikeness. It makes you more like Jesus. How does this happen? It's an inside job! The Bible actually changes your heart.

So what can you do to make sure you don't miss out on the miracle of a spiritual makeover every single day? Here are a few steps you can take to help you keep going and growing your love for and understanding of the Bible. When you take these steps each day, you are making the choice to make time with God a priority—your Number One priority!

Read It

I could add *just* read it. Start anywhere! The only wrong way to read the Bible is to not read it at all. You can find Bible reading schedules in many Bibles and free online or through your Christian bookstore. I've also included one in the back of this book on pages 237-249.

Study It

If you so much as pick up a pencil and underline as you read, you are studying the Bible! Pray this inspired study-the-Bible prayer as you read: "Open my eyes, that I may see wondrous things from Your law" (Psalm 119:18). And you can always ask others to help you find ways to dig deeper into your Bible. I've put a study guide in the back of this book for this purpose—to help you dig deeper into the truths presented throughout this book.

And here's another great tip—or two: Carry a notebook to church and take notes during church and Bible class. And my favorite? Journal what you are learning. I do this…and my journal is a priceless treasure that allows me to read and relive the discovery of God's truths over and over again. Pick a journal that's beautiful, inspiring, or that makes you happy. And, of course, use a pen with your favorite color of ink!

Hear It

Make sure you get to church. And join a women's Bible study. These are two key ways to regularly hear God's Word taught and explained so you can live it. Both of my daughters move—a lot! And the first things they do in their new location is find a church and find a Bible study to join. This enables them to start making new Christian friends right away.

Memorize It

There is no better way to live God's way than to have His Word in your heart and in your mind—and to follow it! If God's truths are there, He will apply them in your daily life. And He will use them to guide you to make right choices.

And let me just say, you can do it! You can memorize. Any kid in a Bible club memorizes verses every week. One of my granddaughters memorized the book of James when she was 11 years old. As I said, you can do it!

Desire It

You already know the importance of physical food. Well, you need to see the spiritual food of the Bible as having even greater importance. As Job declared, "I have treasured the words of His mouth [God's teaching] more than my necessary food" (Job 23:12).

It's Your Choice

Just think—the Bible is all yours all the time. And it's the ultimate source of truth and power. And it's the ultimate beauty treatment starting from the inside out. And it's the ultimate guide to making right choices. As God's Word makes its way into your heart, it energizes your soul. And another benefit is it changes your views about yourself, other people, and the things that are happening in your life.

Do you want a more rewarding and fulfilling life? Then God has good news for you! You can have it. Your better life is as close and as easy as making the choice to pick up your Bible each day, open it up, and take a few minutes to let God speak directly to you. When you do this, you'll know what to do and how to handle everything that comes along. You'll receive your marching orders from God Himself, right there in His love letter to you—the Bible.

The Best Kind of Studying

If you're a Christian, it makes sense that you'd want to learn as much as you could about Jesus Christ and his Word...Think about it—of all the things you learn in your life, what's the most important?...The most important thing is to know who God is and what he wants you to do in your life. And the more you learn about him, the more you feel secure and have strength for whatever challenges you have to face. Reading the Bible is the best kind of studying!

—Kelli[17]

God's Guidelines for Making Right Choices...About Getting into the Bible

These guidelines will help you proceed through your day, confident that you are seeking to make the right choices.

~ *The Bible keeps you from sin.* "Your word I have hidden in my heart, that I might not sin against You" (Psalm 119:11).

~ *The Bible leads you in the right direction.* "Your word is a lamp to my feet and a light to my path" (Psalm 119:105).

~ *The Bible gives you answers.* "All Scripture is given by inspiration of God, and is profitable for doctrine, for reproof, for correction, for instruction in righteousness" (2 Timothy 3:16).

~ *The Bible works on your heart.* "The word of God is living and powerful, and sharper than any two-edged sword, piercing even to the division of soul and spirit, and of joints and marrow, and is a discerner of the thoughts and intents of the heart" (Hebrews 4:12).

~ *The Bible is your greatest treasure.* "...more to be desired are they [God's words and truths] than gold, yea, than much fine gold; sweeter also than honey and the honeycomb" (Psalm 19:10).

5

Powering Up for a Great Day

*In everything
by prayer and supplication, with thanksgiving,
let your requests be made known to God.*
—Philippians 4:6

*H*ere's a prayer experience I'll never forget!

I pulled out a tissue and dabbed my eyes, then patted my nose (trying to be a lady, of course) as I sat on the threadbare couch in our tiny living room and tried to hold myself together. I looked around and surveyed what ten years as a Christian family had provided materially. When my husband, Jim, had sensed a call into the ministry, we had joyfully sold all to follow Christ. With the proceeds, our little family of four had moved into a very small but adequate home so we could better afford to pay for Jim's seminary training while holding down several part-time jobs.

And there I sat, perched on the filthy edge of our old sofa which had, by default, become my "prayer place"! As I looked up to begin my trek through my pages of prayer requests, I caught my daily glimpse of our rain-stained ceiling where the "cottage cheese" finish had once been. We had a leak—it was obvious! And we needed a new roof in the worst way.

But, "Oh, Lord!" my heart cried out, even before I began formal prayer, "there's no money set aside for such a huge expense." I was desperate on that memorable day, because the night before had been a sleepover for our daughters and their church friends. A delightful group of girls had camped out in the living room. And, unfortunately and embarrassingly, in the middle of the night some substance from the ceiling near the main fount of the leak had given in to gravity and the unthinkable had happened. Bits of the ceiling had fallen on the girls as they slept in their carefully lined-up sleeping bags on the living room carpet! Jim and I were shocked awake by the squeals of a scared bunch of ten-year-old girls! (I'm sure the girls and their families still have lots to talk about as they recall their sleepover at the George's!)

Well, as I said, there I was, bawling my eyes out. Not over a lack of "stuff." And not due to the oldness and mold-ness of our "second-hand chic" stuff. And not because of a threadbare couch. And not because of a gaping dark hole in our ceiling. Oh, we'd had stuff for a long time! We had it all! We just hadn't had Christ.

But on that morning—and it's hard to explain—my tears were tears of joy. Why? Because I now had a relationship with the Good Shepherd who promised I would never want or lack for anything I truly needed (see Psalm 23:1). And that's why I was meeting with Him that day in prayer. As a new believer I had learned to stop throwing vague prayers upward and wishing for things like a new roof. Instead, I was learning that I needed to pray specifically for family members, for others, and for missionaries…and for divine intervention regarding the hole in our ceiling!

God Is Available to You—24/7!

My favorite daily writing uniform is a pair of denim cargo pants with six large pockets. In fact, once they became a favorite, I purchased several other colors in the same style. And my most-used pocket on these pants is the one that rides low on my thigh and is large enough to hold my cell phone. Now, even though I have a cell phone, I don't use it nearly as much as my husband, daughters, and other women I know use theirs. For me, its main use is texting my family, reading on my Kindle app (whenever I'm stuck waiting somewhere), making an occasional call, using Twitter, and catching the daily news headlines.

Everyone seems to have a cell phone. And many are opting to have their cell phone replace a home phone. You can be in touch worldwide and at the same time get email and have Facebook, Twitter, and Skype options available. And you can search for information, check your banking accounts, shop online, and purchase just about anything right on your cell phone. It's a wonderful tool and blessing—if you have it with you, if you have it charged, and if you have it turned on. And another blessing is there are very few places where you cannot make and receive a call.

In many ways, your prayer life is like a cell phone—you can pray anytime you want, anywhere you want, for as long as you want. But unlike a mobile phone, prayer has no fees or roaming charges. You also never have to scroll through a directory to find God's number. And your communication with God requires no earpiece, speakerphone, or Bluetooth—it's "hands free." Plus you have a direct line to the God of the universe 24/7/365— 24 hours a day, 7 days a week, 365 days a year. How's that for technology? Divine technology, that is!

Choosing to Pray

Yet for some reason, even though we have this unique, miraculous, direct line to God, we have a hard time making the choice to pray. I had a serious discussion with a group of women just this past Sunday. You see, I am part of a thrilling Sunday school class made up of women at all ages and stages of life. We have newlyweds as well as women in their eighties. We have single women, military wives whose husbands are deployed, professional career women, and stay-at-home moms. This past Sunday we shared our way through a lesson on prayer. At last we got down to discussing different kinds of prayer, followed by talking about what it is that keeps us from praying.

One hundred percent of my classmates agreed that prayer is harder to fit in on a daily basis than spending time reading the Bible. We even dared to share our "cop-out prayers," those prayers in which we ask God's blessing on our day and loved ones with a general, all-encompassing sentence like, "God bless me and my family today."

Next we shared about general "fix-it prayers," usually uttered while saying grace with a meal.

And of course every one of us related to the ever-popular "on-the-go prayer" while driving or starting up the washing machine or standing in line at the grocery store. This easy prayer practice does have its good points—like praying for those involved in a car wreck that's holding up traffic, or for a child who is taking a tough exam, or for difficult tasks our husbands face, or even for our aging and ailing parents.

This is all good!

But at the same time, all of us agreed that stopping the craziness and pressure of our busy days and sitting down in a quiet or secluded place to take time to do one thing and one thing only—pray—was an extremely difficult challenge, not to mention a source of daily failure. Yet considering that the activity of prayer is as easy as bowing your head and simply sharing your heart with God, you would think we would pray a lot more often and faithfully than we do.

10 Reasons We Don't Pray

Have you ever thought about why you don't pray—or pray more? I'm sure you have, and maybe even every day when you don't pray. And so have I. As I look at my own heart and life, I've discovered some reasons—and excuses—for not praying. Here's my list. Maybe you'll find yourself in some of these reasons.

1. *Worldliness*—Our world affects us more than we think. It exerts a constant pressure on us to conform and live like the world lives, instead of living God's way with a full-out passion for Him. And sometimes, in our pride and smugness, because we have food, clothing, shelter, a savings account, family, friends, and lots of fun things to do, we wrongly decide, "Why do I need to talk to God? I've got everything I need without wasting my time praying."

2. *Busyness*—Another reason we don't pray is because we don't take the time or make an effort to pray. Prayer isn't a priority for us, so we fill our time with other seemingly more important things. We're so busy we don't even get around to planning the act of praying into our daily life!

3. *Foolishness*—Whenever we're consumed with what's foolish, trivial, and meaningless, we fail to pray. We begin to lose our ability to know the difference between

what is good and what is evil. Between what is essential and that which has little eternal value. Everything becomes a gray area which doesn't require prayer. (Or so we think!)

4. *Distance*—We have no problem talking with our family and friends. In fact, we could talk for hours—and sometimes we do! But talk to someone outside your circle? Or a visitor at church? Or the new woman at Bible study? That takes a little more effort. It's the same with talking to God. When your relationship with Him isn't maintained and nurtured regularly, you feel like you are talking to a stranger and find it hard to talk to your heavenly Father. You're tongue-tied! Amazingly you just don't know what to say, and you don't feel close to Him or comfortable in His presence. In short, it's awkward!

5. *Ignorance*—We're clueless about how prayer works. And we don't understand how it helps or fits into our relationship with God and making right choices. In essence, we don't really understand God's love for us and His power to make our lives better.

6. *Sinfulness*—We don't pray because we know we've done something wrong. In our hearts we know we need to talk to God about it, confess it, agree with Him that what we did goes against His will and desires for us. What can we do about our sins and failures? Make a choice to keep short accounts with God. Deal with any sin as it comes up—on the spot—at the moment that we slip up and fail.

7. *Faithlessness*—We don't really believe in the power of prayer. That's because we don't know the dazzling promises God has made to us about prayer. We don't know about—or believe—His assurances of answered prayer. Therefore we don't think prayer makes any difference. So…we don't pray.

8. *Pridefulness*—Prayer shows our dependence on God. When we fail to pray, in our pride we're saying that we don't have any needs. Or worse, we're saying, "God, I'm good on this. I've got it covered. I'll take care of myself, thank You very much!"

9. *Inexperience*—We don't pray because…we don't pray! And because we don't pray, we don't know how to pray…so we don't pray! We're like a dog chasing after its tail. It's a cycle that leads nowhere!

10. *Laziness*—Maybe this last reason we don't pray is the chief obstacle. We simply can't or won't put out the effort to talk to God. Prayer is an act of the will. It's a choice—a choice you can know is always a right choice! You have to *want* to do it…and *choose* to do it.[18]

A Handful of Reasons We Should Pray

Think again about Reason #5—ignorance. I don't know about you, but the last thing I want to be is ignorant! Especially ignorant about God and His character and promises. And I'm thinking you don't either.

So, to get started on knowing more about what God teaches about prayer, enjoy and chew on these sparkling promises and assurances about prayer. Especially note God's message to your heart regarding your life, and how prayer helps you live it God's way. Then pick a favorite verse to memorize. And if you don't find one here you like, choose another. God will use it to encourage your faithful attention. Count on it! And He will use it to nurture your commitment to develop within you the heart of a woman who prays.

> Ask, and it will be given to you; seek, and you will find; knock, and it will be opened to you. For everyone who asks receives, and he who seeks finds, and to him who knocks it will be opened (Matthew 7:7-8).

> I say to you, whatever things you ask when you pray, believe that you receive them, and you will have them (Mark 11:24).

> Call to Me, and I will answer you, and show you great and mighty things, which you do not know (Jeremiah 33:3).

> Let us therefore come boldly to the throne of grace, that we may obtain mercy and find grace to help in time of need (Hebrews 4:16).

> Is anyone among you suffering? Let him pray (James 5:13).

> If any of you lacks wisdom, let him ask of God, who gives to all liberally and without reproach, and it will be given to him (James 1:5).

> Love your enemies…and pray for those who spitefully use you and persecute you (Matthew 5:44).

You lust and do not have…because you do not ask.
You ask and do not receive, because you ask amiss,
that you may spend it on your pleasures (James
4:2-3).

Time for a Heart Checkup

Prayer is a spiritual activity. And everyone who has developed a meaningful prayer life will tell you that praying takes a heart decision and requires effort. So, if you're not praying— or not praying very much…or as much as you would like!— run through this checklist. Dare to put your heart through its paces. And to get you started on your heart check-up, echo King David's heart cry to the Lord, "Search me, O God, and know my heart" (Psalm 139:23).

Check your relationship with God. Is there something that's caused a barrier to develop between you and Him? Are you feeling distant from Him? Then ask yourself, "Is there some activity or attitude in my heart that is hindering my relationship with God? Am I sensing the Holy Spirit's conviction that something I'm doing is wrong, or that I've made some choice that's wrong? That I'm behaving in a wrong way—a way that displeases God?"

If the answer is yes, be willing to quickly do whatever it takes to deal with and shatter the obstacles that stand between you and a loving, open relationship with God—one that enables you to talk to Him about anything and everything, including making right choices. After all, if you can't talk to God about the choices you must make, and you can't talk over your options with Him, and you can't ask for His clear leading and guidance, you probably won't be able to make right choices.

Check your lifestyle. Do you attend a church that spurs your spiritual growth, your hunger for God? That teaches biblical truth and the good things of the Lord? And what—or who— is influencing you? Are they influencing you positively for the things of God? If not, they have to go. Also, does your lifestyle include interaction with other Christians who are pushing and pulling you forward in your walk with God? Propelling your growth in Christ? Remember this truth: Nothing and no one is important enough to be allowed to endanger your relationship with God and your ability to talk to Him in prayer.

Check your desire. Prayer will never become a life-changing habit or spiritual discipline if the one main ingredient—desire— is missing. You can know *what* you should do. And you can know *why* you should do it. You can even know *how* to do it. But if you don't *desire* to do it and don't want to do it, you won't choose to do it, and it won't become real in your life. Please, don't let this happen to you when it comes to the choices you make.

Helping Prayer Happen

It's always good to read books about prayer and learn about different ideas and methods for how to make prayer happen. But ultimately, it comes down to your willingness to making it happen. With that in mind, here are two extremely simple principles (more choices!) that will help you overrule any excuses for not praying. These two practices will help you become a woman of prayer.

Head to bed. (And now we are back to Choice #1—getting out of bed.) To get up tomorrow and ensure you have time to pray means you must head to bed tonight at a set time. Here's how it goes. Getting up in time to talk over your life and your problems with God starts by thinking about getting ready for bed as soon as dinner is over. Finish tidying things up, getting kids settled or into bed. Take care of any must-do activities.

Then do all your pre-bed stuff. Wash your face, brush your teeth (you know the drill). Next, check your schedule for tomorrow and begin a to-do list for your bright new day-to-come. Set out your Bible and prayer list or notebook in the place where you plan on having your quiet time the next morning. Then go to bed as early as possible so you can meet and talk with the most important person in your life in the morning—your heavenly Father.

Start a personal prayer notebook. Go ahead and be creative. Make it yours. Choose a favorite color. Decorate it. Add plastic sleeves for photos of those you are praying for. Keep a special pen inside it, and a tissue or two, along with some extra pieces of paper. Then, of course, show up for some real prayer and put that nifty notebook to good use!

Do you remember I said that in the past my prayer time consisted of something like me muttering, "God, bless my family today?" Well, why not be specific—and bold? Why not ask God to bless your husband's efforts at his new job? Or ask Him to bless your daughter's preparations for her SAT exam this Saturday? Or faithfully entreat God to intervene in someone's divorce proceedings? These are specifics, and your notebook pages, which include the people in your life and the concerns you have, can help you with the specifics to be prayed about when you settle down to talk to—or battle with—God about them. Hey, you're probably worrying about those things anyway! So why not take these specific concerns to the Lord each day in prayer?

"Something is better than nothing." This is one of the little motivational talks on prayer I give to myself, along with, "Any prayer is better than no prayer," and "Some prayer is better than none." So start out on your "something," "any," and "some" praying. Start with a choice to pray a few minutes each morning. Then graduate little by little to more time spent in prayer. I personally use a timer. When I first tackled the spiritual discipline of prayer, I would make myself sit down at my kitchen table. Then I set my kitchen timer for five minutes, and gave myself permission to stop when the timer rang.

What happened? The hardest part, of course, was starting. Like everything else, the hardest part of any task is getting started! I couldn't believe how difficult it was to stop all my busyness, turn my back on undone work, turn my mind off to all the work that still had to be done, sit down, set the timer, and (sigh... finally!) start praying.

What I discovered was that once I settled myself into the actual act of praying, I about jumped out of my skin when the timer announced my five minutes was up. Then, because I had already done the hardest part—making a decision to pray and actually starting to pray—all I wanted to do was keep on praying! I was off and running—or off and praying—and having a marvelous time with my Lord.

Think about it. Is five minutes of prayer better than no minutes of prayer? Of course! Something is better than nothing. So start small, and watch for mighty things to happen. Be faithful to lay your decisions-to-make and choices-to-make before God in prayer, and He will be faithful to lead and guide you to making right choices. It's a fact: "In all your ways acknowledge Him, and He shall direct your paths" (Proverbs 3:6).

Stepping Boldly into Your Day

After prayer, you can approach your day with a "Bring it on!" attitude.

How is this possible? Because, by the time you get up from

your prayer time, you've already made many important decisions. You brought your prayer list before the throne of God Himself. Like King Hezekiah of the Old Testament, who took an invading army's written demands and his fears and concerns into the temple and laid them out before God (2 Kings 19:14-19), you too can lay out your issues before God. You can lift up each decision, trial, burden, responsibility, and heartache to God for His holy, righteous, wise input. He is waiting to hear you ask, and wanting to give you His perfect guidance.

Like a changed—or transformed—woman, when you rise up from your time of prayer, you are ready to step out on your path for the day. You are calm. Prayer does that for you because every thing and every issue, no matter how large or small, has been laid into God's lap. You've talked over your relationships with the God of the entire universe and settled with Him on how to handle any problems—at least for today. You've talked over your behavior and your habits with God. And you've received His nod of approval—or His directions for change and improvement.

Can you handle yet another blessing? Because you've checked in with God, you now have an open-line conversation going with Him that can last all day long. You've opened your heart and the door for ongoing communication. So when any surprise, curveball, unexpected news, tragedy, or ill treatment comes along during the day, all you have to do is keep right on talking to God as you walk right on through your trial. You never miss a step in your walk with the Lord when you look to Him immediately. He will instantly guide you in the right way to act and in what to do and say.

In every situation that comes up as the hours pass by, let your heart reach up to the Lord first thing, before you say or do anything. Like James 1:5 instructs, "If any of you lacks wisdom, let him ask of God, who gives to all liberally and without reproach, and it will be given to him." There is no need or reason to miss a single beat in your walk with God if you keep on talking things over with Him throughout the day. As one of my pastors constantly reminded our congregation, "Every breath breathed in should be exhaled in a prayer to God."

So be bold—in your prayers and your faith in God! At any time—through your day and through your life—you can "come boldly to the throne of grace, that [you] may obtain mercy and find grace to help in time of need" (Hebrews 4:16). Follow the example of God's great statesman Nehemiah, and choose to pray!

Nehemiah's Prayer Life

- When discouraged, he prayed (Nehemiah 1:4).
- When searching for direction, he prayed (1:5-11).
- When seeking assistance, he prayed (2:1-5).
- When under attack, he prayed (4:4-5,9).
- When weak and powerless, he prayed (6:9).
- When joyful, he prayed (12:27,43).[19]

God's Guidelines for Making Right Choices...About Prayer

These guidelines will help you proceed through your day, confident that you are seeking to make the right choices.

~ *Determine to obey God's Word*—"If anyone turns a deaf ear to the law, even his prayers are detestable" (Proverbs 29:9 NIV).

~ *Let God know about all your concerns*—"Certainly God has heard me; He has attended to the voice of my prayer. Blessed be God, who has not turned away my prayer, nor His mercy from me!" (Psalm 66:19-20).

~ *Always pray in times of trouble*—"The eyes of the LORD are on the righteous, and His ears are open to their cry...The righteous cry out, and the LORD hears, and delivers them out of all their troubles" (Psalm 34:15,17).

~ *Pray instead of worrying*—"Be anxious for nothing, but in everything by prayer and supplication, with thanksgiving, let your requests be made known to God; and the peace of God, which surpasses all understanding, will guard your hearts and minds through Christ Jesus" (Philippians 4:6-7).

~ *Don't forget to pray for others*—"...praying always with all prayer and supplication in the Spirit, being watchful to this end with all perseverance and supplication for all the saints" (Ephesians 6:18).

6

Living More Like Jesus

*Walk in the Spirit, and you shall not
fulfill the lust of the flesh.*
—Galatians 5:16

All right! You're up. So what if it seems *really* early? And so what if it takes you a while to stagger around and make a cup of coffee or tea? So what if your first foggy minutes are used doing no-brainer tasks like opening the doors to cool down the house (while the coffee is brewing), turning on the computer (while the coffee is brewing some more), and unloading the dishwasher from dinner last night (while the coffee is sputtering away in its grand finale)?

Just keep moving. I call it "puttering time." Go ahead and congratulate yourself for just being up and on the move, be it ever so slow. Sure, you're probably not exactly achieving your lifetime goals…yet. You're not writing a chapter or doing the taxes or finishing up your schoolwork. You're not organizing your daughter's wedding or your parents' fiftieth wedding anniversary celebration or the carpool schedule. You're not scheduling out the next vacation or researching airline ticket prices. No, you are just up and easing into the gift of a brand new day.

But once things get going—and you get that cup of coffee—you must begin. Now you have a big choice to make: Do I let my busy day—no, not my busy day, but my impossible day, my never-get-it-all-done day—drag me down into the pit of despair? Or do I choose to "walk" as in "walk in the Spirit" (Galatians 5:16)? And this, my friend, is a choice. As a Christian, the Bible commands us to "walk in the Spirit." And, as with every command, that also means we can choose *not* to walk in the Spirit.

What It Means to Walk in the Spirit

Now, at this point you might be wondering, *What does all this information about walking in the Spirit have to do with the choices I'm facing? Doesn't the lady know I'm at a crisis-crossroads today? Why isn't she telling me how to choose a college, or a career path, or how to determine a suitable roommate? And how will I know who to marry? (Brad is so cute!) And once I have kids, should I homeschool them?*

The list of choices women must make goes on and on: How to choose a church. When to follow or not follow her husband's wishes. What to do with regard to birth control.

I know all about these situations, and more. I've had to make choices about parents with cancer and parents failing in their nineties. I know about the scary stuff teens face and get into. I've lived through financial insecurity and having to decide whether to get a job or stay home, or whether to quit a job and go home!

So the big question you may be thinking is, *How does walking in the Spirit help me solve my problems and help me make right choices?* Well, I'm glad you asked! For therein lies the secret to making right choices. When you walk in the Spirit, you have God's Holy Spirit guiding and instructing you. He is by your side as your helper as you make your decisions (see John 14:26). With the assurance of God's guiding hand, you'll be well on your way and more confident as you tackle your options.

But maybe I've gotten a little ahead of myself. Maybe a more basic question you are thinking is, *What does it mean to walk in the Spirit?* When you choose to walk in the Spirit, your life, speech, actions, and reactions will be marked by what is referred to in the Bible as "the fruit of the Spirit." Galatians 5:22-23 lists nine qualities, characteristics, or attributes—or "fruit"—that show the whole watching world that you are in tune with God, that you are choosing to handle your day's situations His way:

> The fruit of the Spirit is love, joy, peace, longsuffering, kindness, goodness, faithfulness, gentleness, self-control.

Now let me quickly say that walking in the Spirit does not mean you pretend that your impossible day is not lurking just outside your door. No, it means drawing upon the resources God provides for you to handle your impossible day—to handle it His way, to flow graciously, gracefully, and by His grace through your day with His strength and power...yet relaxed, calm, and in control with evidence of His peace, gentleness, and self-control.

Doesn't this sound like a great solution to your potentially stressful day? Isn't this a great way to tackle—or walk into—your challenging day? Instead of getting angry or pulling out your hair, you smile with joy and wondering anticipation as you wait to see how God will assist you as, together, you and He work through your seemingly impossible day.

Throughout the Bible, the word "fruit" refers to evidence of what is within. Any person who has received Jesus as Savior and Lord and has Christ living within him or her will evidence this fruit. It's called "the fruits of righteousness" (Philippians 1:11). The fruit of the Spirit has been described as "those gracious habits which the Holy Spirit produces in the Christian."[20]

Here are a few facts you need to know about the fruit of the Spirit:

—The list of these "gracious habits" is found in Galatians 5:22-23. To repeat, they are love, joy, peace, patience, kindness, goodness, faithfulness, gentleness, and self-control.

—Every fruit of the Spirit is commanded in Scripture. We are told—not asked—to "walk in the Spirit" (verse 16).

—Every fruit of the Spirit, because it is commanded, therefore requires a decision, a choice: "Will I or won't I choose to walk in the Spirit, to handle this situation, incident, or problem God's way?"

—Every fruit of the Spirit is illustrated in Jesus' life. Walking in the Spirit means being controlled by the Spirit. Jesus walked moment by moment in and by the Spirit. Therefore His life was habitually and totally and perfectly characterized by the fruit of the Spirit.

A Quick Walking Tour of the Fruit

As we take a brief look at the fruit spoken of in Galatians 5:22-23, I believe you'll discover just how their evidence in your life will guide you toward making right choices!

Love is "the sacrifice of self." This simple definition crystalizes what the Bible teaches about love. "Love is not an emotion. It is an act of self-sacrifice. It is not necessarily feeling love toward a particular person. It may not have any emotion connected with it."[21]

Romans 5:8 tells us "God demonstrates His own love toward us, in that while we were still sinners, Christ died for us." From this verse we can see no emotion, but we can sure see that God's love involved sacrifice!

Every fruit of the Spirit requires decisions, choices, and love is no different. It's hard to love under stressful and less-than-ideal conditions. Yet God asks you to choose to...

> give love when you want to withhold,
> reach out to others when you are tired and want to rest,
> serve when you want to be served, and
> help others when you yourself are hurting.

Joy is "the sacrifice of praise." When life is good, praise and thanksgiving flow freely from our hearts and lips. We are cruising along on top of the world! And it's true—when the sun is shining brightly in our hearts and lives, we are so incredibly happy.

But when life turns black and stormy, outbursts of praise and thanksgiving don't flow quite so easily, do they?

This is exactly where people confuse spiritual joy and the emotion of happiness. You see, happiness is an emotion that you feel when you are experiencing good fortune and success. However, you experience spiritual joy when you choose to follow God's advice and "in everything give thanks; for this is the will of God in Christ Jesus for you" (1 Thessalonians 5:18).

Joy is like this: Although you may not *feel* like praising the Lord or thanking Him for what's happening in your life, you go ahead and *choose* to do what God says and lift praise to Him. In spite of your circumstances, you make the effort—you choose!— to be thankful. That's why joy is called a sacrifice. When you'd rather bask in self-pity or stay stuck in your depression, you choose to look beyond your pain and offer up your praise as a sacrifice to God. You choose to focus on *Him*, not on *them*—not on all your problems.

Peace is "the sacrifice of trust." You and I make the sacrifice of trust when we face pain and stress in our lives and choose to trust God instead of panicking or falling apart. When circumstances in your life might push your emotions to stampede in panic, your heart to collapse in terror, your strength to twist into a bundle of nerves, or your mind to be filled with dread, you have a choice to make. You can choose to give in to these feelings and tendencies, or you can choose to trust in God, to present yourself to Him so He can fill you with His peace.

Choosing to trust God—making the sacrifice of trust—causes you to experience His peace even in the midst of tremendous upheaval and chaos. The apostle Paul shows us how to give the sacrifice of trust: "Be anxious for nothing, but in everything by prayer and supplication, with thanksgiving, let your requests be made known to God; and the peace of God, which surpasses all understanding, will guard your hearts and minds through Christ Jesus" (Philippians 4:6-7).

What easy instructions! Do you realize the simplicity of the command? "Be anxious for *nothing!*" Then, once you come to a screeching halt on your anxieties and get that first step out of the way, maybe like me you wonder, *Okay. Check. I've got it, Lord. Now what? What's Step 2?*

Well, here it is. Paul didn't leave us clueless. "In *everything* by prayer and supplication, with thanksgiving, let your requests be made known to God." In other words, *pray!* There's our key to trusting God. Stop worrying...and start trusting. Stop worrying...and start praying.

And then, like whipped cream slathered on top of a warm piece of apple pie or a hot fudge sundae, you will enjoy the abundance of the rich blessing of "the peace of God," which surpasses *all* comprehension and also stands guard over your heart and your mind against fear, anxiety, doubt, and depression. You'll not only *walk* through your trials, you'll sail through them!

Patience chooses to "do nothing." Sometimes I wish the whole idea of patience wasn't in my Bible—and that it wasn't there so *many* times! But it is. And it is God's voice of wisdom telling me (and you) to be patient. He instructs us to "put on" patience—or l-o-n-g-suffering (Colossians 3:12), much like we put on clothes each day.

There's no doubt about it—patience is a tall order. You've probably heard the joke, "Lord, I need patience, and I need it right now!" Maybe you've even uttered this prayer. But we do need God's patience, which has the ability to wait and wait for a very long time! And, as you know, that is next to impossible... without God's help.

But patience isn't only about waiting. It is also key in all relationships, a practical first step to getting along with people. For instance, you are to choose to be patient with your adversaries and difficult or problem people. And you must also choose to wait and practice self-restraint when you are tempted to overreact to the antics and behavior of your children at all ages and stages.

And a best first step toward patience? It is to do nothing. This doesn't mean you won't eventually do something. And it doesn't mean you shouldn't do something. It just means your first response to a stressing situation is to not react, to not scream, to not yell in anger, to not lose your temper.

And the neat thing is that your pause can be a mere second or two during which you put on the brakes and check yourself. A moment when you stop and do nothing for precious seconds that buy you the opportunity to check in with God, to pray a quick-as-lightning prayer, before you do anything. Sometimes patience means taking an hour, or a day, or a week, or maybe even longer, to think and pray and seek counsel *before* you respond to someone, before you make a decision about how to handle a problem.

Believe me, when it comes to making choices, patience is your best friend! So be on guard throughout your day. It's always easy to react negatively or emotionally to a surprise situation or painful event—that's natural! But to act in patience is the harder choice—which is *super*-natural, which is the fruit of the Spirit. When you are patient, you are exhibiting Christlike conduct.

Picture this, if it helps. As I'm thinking about patience, I'm recalling how important it was to teach my children that, in any emergency, they were to rush to the phone and dial 9-1-1. *Then* they were to go get a neighbor, or call a parent, or try to do something about the crisis.

So, as you grapple with growing in patience, think of the first seconds of any difficult encounter as your emergency. Then take the set-in-concrete first step—lift up your 9-1-1 prayer to God. Tell Him your problem. Ask for His help. Ask for His patience. And while you're at it, ask Him for His wisdom too! Take care of this all-important first response—your 9-1-1 emergency response. *Then* begin to handle your situation.

Kindness chooses to "plan to do something." While patience does nothing rash and sinful while resisting in patience, kindness plans to act. Kindness, like all the other fruit of the Spirit, desires godly action and, therefore, *chooses* to look for opportunities to do something. Kindness is tenderness and concern for other people. It involves having a sweetness of disposition. And it is a matter of the heart.

Surely you and I can look through eyes of love and a heart of compassion, and choose to do something for those around us—especially those who make our lives difficult. Here's a thought: Why not create a section in your prayer notebook entitled "Enemies"? Whenever you have a challenging relationship, or you have an unpleasant or stressful encounter with someone, this situation goes on this list. Then each day you can pray and plan for kindness. You see, kindness is part of your walk with God! You don't want to allow any person or situation to mar or disrupt your relationship and communion with Him. Prayer helps to keep your heart right with God and your relationships handled His way.

Goodness chooses to "do everything." Oh, how I love this fruit of the Spirit! Goodness does everything it can to shower God's blessings upon others. Goodness follows through on the wonderful thoughts of kindness. Goodness takes the giant step from good intentions to actually doing everything it can to serve others.

John Wesley, the famous preacher of a few centuries ago, understood this principle of doing everything. In fact, he chose to make it a rule for his life, putting it into practice in the following ways:

> Do all the good you can,
> by all the means you can,
> in all the ways you can,
> in all the places you can,
> in all the times you can,
> to all the people you can,
> as long as ever you can.

Surely, if this man could choose to exhibit this sort of kindness, without distinguishing between friend or foe, you too can choose to put kindness on your daily to-do list.

Faithfulness chooses to "just do it." This could be my favorite fruit of the Spirit. Maybe that's because I was so lost and remedial in being a self-starter, a finisher, one who accomplished goals and diligently took care of others—like my husband and children! My definition of faithfulness says it all: Faithfulness means "just do it."

And as a fruit of the Spirit, faithfulness means *choosing* to do it…no matter what. And doing it regardless of feelings, moods, or desires—if the Lord wills (James 4:15).

"Do it" should become your battle cry as you struggle each day with whatever your special areas of weakness are. For instance, tiredness heads the list for most of the women I know and communicate with, followed closely by laziness. But when you make a decision to *do it*, and you choose to look to God for His strength and purpose in *doing it*, He gives you the grace to have victory over tiredness and laziness, or whatever your special problem areas are.

And this one character quality of faithfulness will set you in a remarkable and wonderful category of women. Sadly, it is such a rarity in our world! By choosing to be faithful you will be living out one of God's instructions to His women—that we are to be "faithful in all things" (1 Timothy 3:11).

"Faithful in all things." How would you like these words on your tombstone? Better than that is, how would you like them written in the hearts, minds, and memories of those who know you and are blessed by your reliable friendship and ministry? No price can be set for the value of a faithful servant of the Lord, a faithful wife or mom or grandmom, a faithful sister and in-law, and a faithful friend.

Gentleness chooses to "take it." Gentleness, or as it's sometimes translated, meekness, is like all the other fruit of the Spirit. You must look to God for it because there is no other way to respond and display it. Gentleness grows from trusting the Lord with what is happening—or not happening—in your life. A woman who is characterized by gentleness finds her refuge and strength in the Lord. This strong faith and trust enables her to endure unkind behavior and suffering knowing she belongs to an all-knowing, all-wise, caring Father and trusting fully in His love.

A well-known and much-loved verse in 1 Peter shows you and me God's perspective on the beauty of gentleness, especially in His women. Rather than paying too much attention to your outward appearance, God tells you to be consumed with taking meticulous care to adorn "the hidden person of the heart, with the incorruptible beauty of a gentle and quiet spirit, which is very precious in the sight of God" (3:4).

In the eyes of the world, gentleness may look like weakness. But gentleness is like velvet-covered steel. Because of a woman's firm, unshakeable faith and trust in God (the steel), she is able to respond to challenges and pain with gentleness (the velvet). It requires more strength to be gentle than it does to lose your temper, talk back, fight, or have a fit!

Self-control chooses "not to do it." It's a fact: You and I live in a world that desires to press you into its mold, to "conform" you to its image (Romans 12:2). Temptations surround you on every front. Yet, in times of temptation, a woman who walks by the Spirit chooses "not to do it," not to succumb to the pressure and the ways of the world.

In other words, you choose not to give in to emotions, to cravings, to urges. You choose not to think or do what you know is against God's Word. You choose not to pamper yourself, thinking you deserve it. You refuse to choose the easy way out. When it comes to sin and compromise, you choose not to rationalize such conduct—and there are thousands of other "don't do its"!

In short, self-control is looking to God for His strength and grace to say no to whatever you must reject to live in Christlike conduct, in a way that meets God's standards.

The Fine Art of Walking

To come full circle to where we started with understanding what it means to walk in the Spirit, in simple terms, walking in the Spirit means choosing to live each moment in submission to God. Walking in the Spirit means seeking to please God with the thoughts you choose to think, the words you choose to say, the actions you choose to take. Walking by the Spirit means letting God guide you each step of the way. It's letting Him work in and through you so that you bring glory to Him.

Of course, you and I both realize that walking by the Spirit isn't easy. I'm sure you've noticed that as a believer who has been born again by the renewing work of the Holy Spirit, you still struggle with sin. You've probably felt like the apostle Paul who stated, "I know that nothing good dwells in me, that is, in my flesh" (Romans 7:18 NASB). He bemoaned the fact that "the good that I will to do, I do not do" (verse 19). I'm sure you've been there and done that! So, what's the solution? How can you get the upper hand in the battle that rages between your Spirit and your flesh? The secret is called "abiding in Christ," which will again require some choices on your part. (See "God's Guidelines for...Living More Like Jesus" on page 96).

Choosing to Grow in Godliness

It is a tragedy when Christians don't grow much beyond their initial spiritual birth. Yes, they say they are Christians, but they seem to habitually make wrong choices, and therefore, they habitually exhibit just small evidences of fruit. They produce small pieces of something that looks more like raisins. Oh, it's fruit, but it's dry, shriveled up, and not very pretty!

God wants you to flourish—to blossom and bloom! To exhibit lush, mature spiritual fruit, to "grow in the grace and knowledge of our Lord and Savior Jesus Christ" (2 Peter 3:18). Therefore, you have another choice to make: Do you want to grow to spiritual maturity? Do you desire to bear much fruit? If so, your spiritual growth will require some tough choices on your part—choices you will need to make day after day, and many times each day. Somehow people manage to choose to do the things that are important to them. So, how important is walking with Jesus to you? Hopefully, it is becoming more and more important!

As you commit to improving your walk with God and making better choices, choose this thoughtful, deliberate, calculated, prayerful, and Spirit-led approach as you move down the path.

One foot in front of the other
One step at a time
One thought at a time
One sentence at a time
One response at a time
One decision at a time
One minute at a time
One day at a time
…for a lifetime
And when you fail, stop it!
Admit it, confess it, apologize for it, and
Go on.

God's Guidelines for Making Right Choices...
Living More Like Jesus

These guidelines will help you proceed through your day, confident that you are seeking to make the right choices.

~ *Choose to stay close to Christ.* "I am the vine, you are the branches. He who abides in Me, and I in him, bears much fruit; for without Me you can do nothing" (John 15:5).

~ *Choose to spend time in God's Word.* "Oh, how I love Your law! It is my meditation all the day. You, through Your commandments, make me wiser than my enemies; for they are ever with me" (Psalm 119:97-98).

~ *Choose to spend time in prayer.* "The effective, fervent prayer of a righteous man [woman] avails much" (James 5:16).

~ *Choose to obey God's commands.* "If you keep My commandments, you will abide in My love, just as I have kept My Father's commandments and abide in His love" (John 15:10).

~ *Choose to deal with sin.* "If we confess our sins, He is faithful and just to forgive us our sins and to cleanse us from all unrighteousness" (1 John 1:9).

7
Making the Most of Your Time

See then that you walk circumspectly, not as fools but as wise,
redeeming the time, because the days are evil.
—Ephesians 5:15-16

How time flies! At least it sure seems that way. In my mind it was only a short time ago that I was struggling to write my first book. Yes, literally writing each and every word by hand. I can still remember going to my local Staples and purchasing a pack of 12 legal-size yellow pads. I used both pens and pencils as I scribbled, wrote, edited, cut (with scissors) and pasted (with tape), rewrote, and rewrote again. My stack of revisions complete with coffee stains and tears of frustration reached to the full height of Freya, our neighbor's good-sized cat!

And now, as I look at the copyright date on my first book, *Loving God with All Your Mind*, I realize that even though it was quite the ordeal, time has had a way of quickly flowing by. Time's passing is like the steady, ever-constant flowing of a great river. Its flow is ever so gentle, yet ever so persistent. And one day you wake up and say, "No—it couldn't have been more than 15 years already!" But there it is, printed in black and white.

Where, I wonder, has the time gone?

The Reality of Time

Have you thought much about time? The 24 hours, the 1440 minutes of your each and every day? As a teen, for me, time had meaning only as it related to the last day of school each year, the first day of school, and then the senior prom—and, of course, the time remaining until I could get my driver's license! During those years of youth it seemed that time couldn't go fast enough for the next milestone in my young life. Time seemed to stand still as I anticipated the next big event! All I had to do was endure each day…and wait.

I'm sure you've heard the expression, "Be careful what you wish for; you just might get it!" Well, all that time that I wished would hurry up and go by as a teen has accelerated to warp speed. I feel like it's whizzing by so fast that I'm breathless and wrung out just trying to hold on to all that's taking place around me.

Now, obviously all this talk of time slowing down or speeding up is only my perception. But I am guessing you know exactly what I mean, and you've experienced it yourself.

So that we can get a better grasp on the concept of time, here are some points I've come to realize over the years:

Time is measured out to each person each day in the same amount.

Time can never be stored for future use.

Time happens only once and then is gone forever.

Time is limited for each person to their life span.

Time is unstoppable.

Time is something that is always in short supply.

Time, when managed and focused properly, produces significant results.

Time is a commodity that can either be redeemed or squandered.

Redeeming the Time

Time is a perishable commodity. And with this commodity, you have only two choices. You can let it slip through your fingers, wasting it, or (my personal favorite expression) "killing" it. Or there is the Bible's option: You can redeem it. This idea of redeeming time is found in Ephesians 5:15-16: "See then that you walk circumspectly [carefully], not as fools but as wise, redeeming the time, because the days are evil."

Friend, in these few verses we are exposed to the ultimate wisdom needed to use our time for the greatest purpose and impact. The apostle Paul wrote 13 books of the New Testament, led three long missionary journeys to establish numerous churches, and preached to untold numbers of people—all of which he accomplished after he reached middle age. How did he do it? Hear him talk you through his take on time:

Guard your walk—Paul warns believers to "see then that you walk circumspectly" (verse 15). The word "circumspectly" is not familiar to most vocabularies, and it basically means being careful, calculated, or, as the verse says, "wise." The secret of making the most of each day is to train yourself to have foresight about what's ahead or around the next corner. To be considering the best and wisest way to manage each situation. To be thinking intelligently about your day, about what decisions you may have to make, and then developing a plan. This kind of preparation will help steer your choices throughout your day and enable you to use your time for profitable results.

Change your attitude—Paul tells us to think and act "not as fools." A foolish woman takes off in all directions at once. She has no plan. She hasn't thought about the day, about how God wants her to live out His will. So, she doesn't make the most of her time. She squanders it, kills it, and has little of value to show for her day when it is done.

That's why it's a good idea to pray each morning, "Lord, I don't want to be a fool today. Help me to remember how important my time is today."

Embrace your goal—There are some things and issues we have to pray for God to reveal to us. But that's not the case when it comes to the use of your time and your day. He tells you! You are to be "redeeming the time." How? You redeem time when you carefully determine what God's will is for your life. As you study, pray, and seek counsel, you become wise and gain understanding. You grow in wisdom. As you obey His will, you redeem or "buy up the opportunities" and don't waste time, energy, money, or talent on anything that is contrary to His will.

Know the reason—God even supplies the reason for redeeming your time. He says it's necessary to do this because "the days are evil." You are to walk wisely and with care because of the evil days we live in. Many are living in sin, and the time is short. So God wants you to make full use of your time to serve as many as possible and to warn others. When you misuse time through lost opportunities, that time can never be regained; those golden minutes with their golden opportunities are gone forever. God is admonishing you to pray, "Oh, Lord! Please help me to use my time wisely—just for today." Then pray this again *every* day!

Numbering Your Days

I absolutely adore every New Year's Day. In fact, I like New Year's even better than my birthday! I go crazy setting up my calendars (yes, that's plural) for my fresh new year. I've used a Planner Pad® for several decades, and still do. I also have two (yes, two) 2x3-foot erasable calendars for two back-to-back years in what my husband and I nicknamed "The War Room." And, of course, I've got sticky notes—in every size, color, and shape—used generously and stuck *every*where!

What kind of calendar (or the plural, calendars) do you use? My Jim is a master at using the calendar supplied by his Internet browser. And he puts the Sticky Notes app on his computer to work for him as well. My daughters are wizards when it comes to utilizing their cell phones—complete with chimes, alarms, and prescheduled reminders—to guide their busy days with busy, buzzing households.

Oh, where would we *be* without our calendars?

But...have you ever heard of a backward calendar? It's a self-made calendar that portrays a countdown of your life. In Psalm 90 the psalmist suggested a general end date for your backward calendar when he wrote, "The days of our lives are seventy years; and if by reason of strength they are eighty years..." (verse 10). According to those numbers, if you are 30 years old, you may have about 40 to 50 years left in your life (or 14,600 to 18,250 days). Or if you are 50, then you can figure you have about 20 to 30 years remaining (or 7300 to 10,950 days).

The psalmist goes on to point out that our days are "soon cut off, and we fly away" (verse 10). In other words, the life of a person is only a brief moment in time. And what is the solution? "Teach us to number our days, that we may gain a heart of wisdom" (verse 12).

Getting Your Act Together

What a wake-up call! God is calling you to stop thinking, *Hey, there's plenty of time left for me to get to my dreams and goals. Right?*

Actually, no. That's a wrong conclusion. Your time is in God's hands. You have no clue what day will be your last. In the meantime, your days are racing forward. They are on a downhill slide and rapidly accelerating like the proverbial snowball that gains momentum as it rolls down a slippery slope!

So with this reality check, what can you do about the choices you are making in connection with the use of your time and your days and your life-focus? I'm hoping you'll join me so that together we can roll up our sleeves and determine how to make our remaining years truly count for Christ.

How about beginning with some stopgaps? That's always a good first choice! You can start by putting the brakes on certain practices and habits that are hindering your best efforts for Christ. What choices can you make to guard against being robbed of any more of your precious minutes? What are the choices you must make to ensure that you keep moving toward God's plans and purposes for you and the days of your life? To get you started, consider these:

1. *Choose to do it now.* Most people are professional procrastinators. They know they should make a decision or confront an issue or complete some task. Yet, because it may be unpleasant, time-consuming, or require a ton of effort, they choose to put it off until the day is over—and as a result, something vital remains left undone. There goes another day, a day that on your countdown calendar you couldn't afford to waste.

The solution that has helped me is to say, "Do it, and do it now." In fact, all through each day, I say to myself, "Elizabeth, just get in there and do it—do anything on it, do it badly, do it slowly. Just do it!"

Here's another tip you might find helpful. Ask yourself, "What is the worst thing that could happen if I do this thing I'm dreading?" Then ask yourself the same question in reverse: "What is the worst thing that could happen if I don't do this thing I'm dreading?"

As you know all too well, in most cases you have probably created some great barrier to moving forward—a barrier that was created with each passing moment of delay, a barrier that could easily have been hurdled if you had just chosen to act and do it!

2. *Choose to make a plan or schedule.* You'll probably hear me say this again in this book: If you don't plan your day, someone else will plan it for you. So, who do you want to plan your precious, never-to-be-replaced days? You're the one who knows the importance of your days. So why let someone else—who is clueless about your goals and your God-given priorities and desires—plan even one 24-hour span of your life? *This*—today—is the day, the fleeting day, that God has given you to serve Him and live for Him. It is all you have for living out His divine plan...until tomorrow. So make another all-important right choice—plan your own day, and plan it early!

3. *Choose to guard your time with people.* God created us to be social beings. We girls love people and love to be with them. And this is normal. But too much time with people can keep you from fulfilling your goals of serving the Lord and doing His work.

There are, of course, the priority people in your life—primarily, your family. These precious ones must be given as much time as they need. But choose to seek God's wisdom when it comes to how much time you spend with the other people who cross paths with you during the day. Some people need your helping hand—and God wants you to give it. Others, however, may simply have no plans of their own, or may be creating a diversion in order to put something off or to get out of doing something, and they would love to have you join them in the poor choices they are making for their day.

I love getting together with people for just about *any* reason just as much as the next woman. But I've had to set some parameters for myself. One of the hardest was realizing that even though as a writer I work at home, that doesn't mean I'm available. I treat my days like a job, marking off 8:00 am to 4:00 pm as work hours. I schedule any appointments for after 4:00, if at all possible.

And another "intruder alert" I try to identify is, "Hey, how would you like to get together for lunch today…go shopping… meet for coffee?" What I try to do is spend a few minutes right then catching up or chatting instead of getting together when there's no issue or problem to discuss. And if there *is* an issue or problem, I go ahead and schedule the get-together at a time that takes into consideration my daily work schedule.

It's hard! Oh, is it ever. I can easily feel guilty for saying no. Worse than that, I can feel as though I'm being deprived of something everyone else is enjoying. But I have to remember that if I were in an office working for an employer, no one would call me for a spontaneous meeting, and everyone would understand!

Here's a solution for both of us. Learn, with each people encounter, to ask God for wisdom. Ask Him how much, if any, time you should spend with each person. Ask Him to spell out what the need of the moment is, and then follow His leading. Ask Him to help you evaluate your commitments and responsibilities for your day. Ask Him if this latest interruption is His plan or something that would derail your prayed-over plan made for your day and the accomplishments you need to make happen.

4. *Choose to multiply your activities.* How do you make this happen? In two words: First, *delegation.* Obviously, you can't delegate to a two-year-old, but as the children get older, start assigning them family chores, making the running of your home a team effort. If you are asked by the women's group at the church to head a team or run a ministry, pray first about who might help you with this responsibility. Try to find others who can help you and shoulder the load together. With the help of others, the job will get done faster, others will learn new skills, and you will have redeemed some time.

There's a second way to multiply yourself. It's called *duplication* of activities. You multiply yourself by doing two things at once, like picking up your clothes from the dry cleaner's while on your way to the grocery store. Or stopping by the grocery store after picking up the kids at school. This becomes a twofer— you accomplish two things at once. And while you are at the grocery store, you can have your kids walk the aisles with you and help retrieve the things on your list. In doing this you also teach them how to do the grocery shopping, waiting for that blessed day when they can do the shopping for you on their way home from school. So, delegate and duplicate. Both are great ways to redeem your time.

5. *Choose to limit time spent on your computer.* The computer is a wonderful tool. You can research and find just about anything! But unfortunately it has become an addiction for many computer-savvy women. With social media sites like Facebook and Twitter, many women are spending more time than they should casually chatting with friends and acquaintances, while

forgetting about the more pressing relationships that live right under their own roof. How are you doing in this area? Over the next few days, log the amount of time you spend surfing the Internet, tweeting, and chatting on Facebook. You might be surprised to discover how many hours you spend on your computer when you have more urgent and higher-priority obligations waiting to be taken care of.

6. *Choose to limit your time on the phone.* Like the computer, the cell phone is a great invention. But also like the computer, it can easily consume a lot more time than we want it to. We talk on the cell phone while walking, eating, working, and even driving (even when the law tells us not to!). Now, talking on a cell phone is a good use of your time while you are waiting in a checkout line, or while you are waiting to have the oil changed in your car. But because a cell phone is *so* convenient, it's easy to let talking on it become second nature, to the point you don't even notice how much time you're spending on it.

The caution comes when the phone becomes an instrument for careless, aimless chatting that ends up becoming malicious gossip. With cell phones, it's easy for women to become "busybodies, saying things which they ought not" (1 Timothy 5:13).

Instead of letting your phone master you, you need to master your phone. Use it for business, keeping up with family, and truly important connections, such as ministry calls. Beyond that, exercise great caution and beware of the destructive power of the little device that's so often connected to your ear.

7. *Choose your reading material carefully.* This questionable material can be in the form of newspapers, junk mail, magazines, novels, and content you find on the Internet. Be careful that these secondary forms of reading don't rob you of time for

the good, the better, the best, and the eternal. Put these activities in their proper place—and that might even include the trash can! Make it a discipline not to spend more time on literature of temporal value than you spend on spiritual pursuits of eternal value, like reading your Bible, memorizing Scripture, and praying. Susanna Wesley, the mother of John Wesley, gives similar advice:

> I will tell you what rule I observed…when I was young, and too much addicted to childish diversions, which was this—never to spend more time in mere recreation in one day than I spend in private religious devotions.[22]

8. *Choose the right priorities.* No one would disagree with how busy you are. Just look at your schedule of activities. You are running all over the place. *Busyness* is your middle name. But busyness is not an indicator of effectiveness. Activity is not synonymous with productivity.

If you are busy choosing the wrong things, then you are robbing yourself of time that could be better spent on the things that truly count—on God-given priorities. That's why it's so important to take time each day to think about what's involved in redeeming the time and numbering your days.

If I'm going to be guilty of wasting time, let it be on a sunny beach somewhere, rather than spending time on pursuits that have very little—if any—eternal value. Choosing your priorities is such an important choice, so we'll spend more time looking at this later on.

The Value of Time

Time seems like an odd subject to be discussing in relation to making right choices, doesn't it? But once you realize how fragile a moment of time is, and how irreplaceable it is, then just maybe it's worth spending a little of your time discussing it. Oh, how I pray that you now have a better appreciation of the value of your time! This little poem says it all:

I have only just a minute,
Only sixty seconds in it...

Just a tiny little minute,
But eternity is in it.

God's Guidelines for Making Right Choices... Choosing to Value Time

These guidelines will help you proceed through your day, confident that you are seeking to make the right choices.

~ *Remember the fragile nature of life*—"LORD, make me to know my end, and what is the measure of my days, that I may know how frail I am" (Psalm 39:4).

~ *Focus on your priorities*—"One thing I do, forgetting those things which are behind and reaching forward to those things which are ahead, I press toward the goal" (Philippians 3:13-14).

~ *Relax in God's timing*—"To everything there is a season, a time for every purpose under heaven" (Ecclesiastes 3:1).

~ *Order your time*—"Let all things be done decently and in order" (1 Corinthians 14:40).

~ *Get a jump on your day*—"She also rises while it is yet night" (Proverbs 31:15).

8

Breaking Your Worry Habit

Be anxious for nothing.
—Philippians 4:6

It's true confession time. I'm a worrywart from way back. In fact, in my earlier days, I could easily have been president of the International Worrywart Society. You could have readily spotted me in a crowd. I was the one with nails bitten down to the quick. The one with the perpetual frown. The one with a package of Tums, popping them on a regular basis. Are you getting the picture? I have some pretty sad tales from my years as a fussbudget. Part of the problem is that I'm a Type A personality, a perfectionist. I don't say that as an excuse—it's just another part of my confession.

It's so easy to find things to worry about. When I saw someone else doing a job or task that needed to get done, I could always see how, if it was done my way, it would get done "right." I preoccupied myself with things I shouldn't have worried about. I was always thinking and brooding, and my mind would usually circle down into a dark hole. I could think up all the calamities that could happen to my girls—including any future unborn grandchildren! These are toxic qualities when mixed with unbelief, and I was a real mess!

As I now understand how bankrupt my life was, I can comprehend how, all things considered, I was only acting out the life of an average unbeliever. At least I had an excuse back then before I met Jesus Christ. Then, when I became a new creation, a new person, and as His child, I had His word telling me, "Do not be anxious about anything" (Philippians 4:6 NIV).

Worrying is a bad habit. Even though Jesus tells me not to worry, it's hard to keep from doing so, having been a major-league worrier in the past. But praise God, I'm now a recovering worrier, thanks to His guiding Spirit. Through it all, I have learned some shocking truths about worry.

The Truth About Worry

Worrying is something we love to do—or at least that's true for most of the women I know! And the things we can worry about are as varied as all the issues and people in our lives and our overactive imaginations. Whatever happens to be on our minds can spark a worry attack.

But wait. I'm getting ahead of myself. Exactly what does the word *worry* mean? When I learned that God's Word instructed me *not* to worry, I decided I should find out why this caution is stated so firmly: "Do not be anxious about anything." So I dug into a number of dictionaries and found these definitions regarding the verb *worry*:

> To feel uneasy, troubled
> To be overcome with a nagging concern
> To be plagued with doubts
> In the biblical sense, *worry* means to have a sinful, willful distraction that pulls your trust away from God. (That's troubling!)
> In a personal sense it means to have an anxiety that you need to unload to God. (That's comforting.)

As I thought about worry and some of the implications these definitions point to, I began to realize why I wasn't supposed to worry. For instance...

> Worry is a response to something that is going on in a person's life.
> Worry is a condition produced when no solution is seen.
> Worry is an activity generated by what seems to be limited options.
> Worry is an action that has no legitimate basis.
> Worry is a condition that affects everyone.
> Worry is a reaction that produces no positive results.
> Worry is positive only where sin is involved.
> Worry is a sin that denies the power of God.

Breaking the Worry Habit...Forever!

Just glancing back through these definitions made me realize that all of life and its challenges can cause us to worry. But for most of our problems, there are solutions that remove the need to worry and allow us to replace worry with action. One immediate solution is to realize the fact that you and I are not alone. Everyone is tempted to want to travel life's road alone. But guess what—and you're going to love this!

God is always present at your side. His Son's death has provided for your sins, and you are now His child. God is watching over you, and He will never leave you. These are sure and totally trustworthy promises. So...why worry?

Even with the assurance of God's presence in our lives, I'm sure you'll agree that worry and worrying still need to be addressed—and conquered and obliterated. Because worry is an affront to God and is counterproductive to you as a person, wouldn't you think that Christians would at least want to banish this activity out of their lives forever? After all, God's care for us is constant. He Himself is the Good Shepherd who assures us we will never lack anything we truly need (Psalm 23:1). And we possess a plethora of promises from Him that He will take care of every facet of our lives.

Even then, sad to say, most Christians (and that includes me) have serious and frequent bouts of worry. There are plenty of opportunities to turn on the worry machine!

So how can a woman who wants "the peace of God, which surpasses all understanding" (Philippians 4:7) break the worry habit and choose not to be anxious?

As a woman who worried big time, I suffered from a bleeding ulcer, colitis, and a nervous rash on my arms up to both elbows. Yes, I went to doctors, and yes, I took medication. Yes, there was improvement. But doctors and pills and salves couldn't remedy my worry habit.

So I turned to God. I read my Bible and prayed for God's help with my worry problem, Suddenly I noticed there were soooo many commands telling me not to worry! Out of the list of "do not worry" verses I grabbed onto two of them. I began pulling them out whenever I felt my stomach begin to burn or tie in knots, or I found myself wondering and worrying.

I'm thrilled to share these verses with you. I know they will help you as much as they have helped me. Pray along with me and begin to willfully make the choice not to worry.

"Do Not Worry"

The first verse is Matthew 6:25. As you read here, you can't help but acknowledge that our Lord has a command—not advice, not a financial tip, not a suggestion, not something for us to think about, but instruction—for us when it comes to worrying about the basics of life. Jesus said:

I say to you, do not worry about your life, what
you will eat or what you will drink; nor about your
body, what you will put on. Is not life more than
food and the body more than clothing?

Here Jesus is teaching His disciples and all those who are
gathered to listen to what is referred to as the Sermon on the
Mount. In the course of this sermon He stated a fact of life: "No
one can serve two masters...You cannot serve God and mammon
[money]" (verse 24).

And His very next statement? It begins with a three-word
command: "Do not worry." Note the force of Jesus' simple yet
direct words in these different translations:

"*Do not* worry about your life" (NKJV).
"*Stop* worrying about your life" (Wms).
"*Do not* be anxious about your life here" (TCNT).
"*Put away* anxious thoughts about [your life]"
(NEB).[23]

Immediately you and I have a problem: To worry about
anything, then, is disobedience to our Lord's express command.
For me and a lot of others, this surely must be one of the most
difficult commands to obey. Yet Jesus explains why we don't
need to worry:

For your heavenly Father knows that you need all
these things. But seek first the kingdom of God
and His righteousness, and all these things shall be
added to you (verses 32-33).

Worry in a believer is equivalent to a lack of faith in God's
ability to provide for his needs. It's actually a choice to believe
that God doesn't have your best interest in mind. Both are an

expression of doubt in God's Word, and ultimately in God Himself. Clearly, this is a contradictory position for a believer to take, as one who has personally experienced God's salvation. As one whom God has clearly said He has adopted as His child. As one to whom God has pledged in His Word that he has a share in His kingdom (verse 33).

This truth makes the Sermon on the Mount so practical. We cannot simultaneously seek God's glory *and* our own security or comfort without being unfaithful to our Lord. He loved us enough to die for us, and He wants us to glorify His Father. The acid test here is this: Do you believe God's promise to care for you, or not?

Jesus' message is crystal clear. It can't be missed or misinterpreted. It's to the point, and is delivered in three simple, understandable words: *Do not worry*. His followers were worrying—they were anxious and overly concerned—about the basics of daily living. They were fretting about food and clothes. So much so that they were losing their focus on God, on 100 percent devotion to Him as they lived out His kingdom priorities. Their service to God (which is of eternal value) was being diluted and was at risk due to their obsession with daily basics (which are temporal and earthly in nature).

Dear friend, it's a fact: Fear and worry will immobilize you in your kingdom work. They will distract you from your worship and love of God. Your service to God and His people—not to mention your personal peace and joy—is hampered and blocked when you worry and fail to trust Him.

This makes worry a serious habit, don't you think?

"Do Not Be Anxious"

The second scripture I learned to turn to when I started worrying was Philippians 4:6-7:

> Be anxious for nothing, but in everything by prayer and supplication, with thanksgiving, let your requests be made known to God; and the peace of God, which surpasses all understanding, will guard your hearts and minds through Christ Jesus.

Notice the command—"Be anxious for nothing." Another version translates this as "Be careful for nothing" (KJV). The original Greek word used here for "anxious" or worry describes being pulled in different directions. The way the apostle Paul used this phrase, "Be anxious for nothing" meant to stop a practice that had been going on habitually. Evidently his readers were worrying on a routine basis.

Next comes the cure—"In everything by prayer and supplication, with thanksgiving, let your requests be made known to God." The cure for worry? Believing prayer. The apostle Paul gives specific details of how prayer is to be used to squelch worry. Notice the four different words he used in reference to prayer:

"Prayer"—speaks of adoration addressed to God as an act of worship and devotion.
"Supplication"—this comes from a word that means to humbly ask for one's personal needs.
"Thanksgiving"—this refers to expressing appreciation and gratitude.
"Requests"—this emphasizes specific requests versus asking in generalities.

The recipient—"Let your request be made known to God." The preposition "to" or "unto" suggests the idea of being in God's presence. The one who is praying needs to understand that God is always present. Therefore, worry is inappropriate, and worry-free requests are always welcome.

The consequence—"The peace of God, which surpasses all understanding, will guard your hearts and minds through Christ Jesus" (verse 7). Whew—at last! We can exhale now. Peace is ours. As you are faithful to pray and cast your cares upon Jesus, He provides assuring peace. His peace is powerful, like a sentinel who stands guard and patrols in front of your heart's door, keeping worry out. This peace does not mean the absence of trials in your life. But it does mean experiencing a quiet confidence in your spirit regardless of whatever difficult circumstances, people, or events you are facing.

God's One Exception

I'm sure you are familiar with the statement, "There's an exception to every rule." Well, here's the exception to Jesus' and Paul's command not to worry. There is one time when worry is a good thing! You should worry about God's will. You should always be concerned that you are making choices that please God, that further His kingdom, that conform to His will. Your constant concern should be the same as the one Jesus prayed in the Garden: "Not as I will, but as You will" (Matthew 26:39).

I'm sure you don't wake up each morning and think, *Hmmm, let me see just how many decisions I can make today that will dishonor God and be an affront to His holiness.* Yet on many days, that's exactly what happens when you don't take your choices more seriously, and especially when you don't take your choices, your decision-making to God. Worry should be the primary motive for making sure you consult with God through His Word, prayer, and the wisdom of godly counsel. If you worry about the rightness of your choice before you make it, then you will experience less remorse because you avoided making a wrong choice.

To repeat, it's a good thing to worry about every choice you are about to make. But pay special attention to those situations where...

> ...your motives are questionable or less than godly, like fear, greed, anger, people-pleasing.
> ...there seem to be no options.
> ...the answer looks like the easier way out.
> ...a quick answer is required.

Doing Your Part

Did you notice I didn't dwell on specific matters we as women are prone to worry about, such as our children, husbands, finances, health, and so on? We could fill libraries with our concerns! No, the real issue is not our specific worries. It's our willingness to place our full trust in the One who can assist us with our worries. Jesus Himself said, "Do not worry." Case closed!

You have so much to be thankful for. To begin, God has promised to be there for you, provide for you, comfort and strengthen you, assist and help you. And then He promises that when this life is finished, He has a place prepared for you, a forever-home in heaven. So rather than worry about things you cannot control, start with what you *can* do. If you are going to worry about anything, it should be about the choices you are making. Are your choices right in the sight of God? How can you make sure you move in that direction? What can you do?

Choose to grow spiritually (2 Peter 3:18). The more you know of God's holiness, the more likely you are to make the most godly choices. The more you know of God's provision, the less likely you are to doubt God's goodness.

Choose to keep a clean slate (1 John 1:9). Sin clouds your judgment, hinders the Spirit's prompting, and sears your conscience. These are only a few of the consequences of sin. So be quick to seek God's forgiveness when you've sinned. You cannot afford to be in sin and out of the will of God, even for a brief moment!

Choose to avoid sinful situations (2 Timothy 2:22). Choose to stay clear of any situation that may cause you to stumble into sin, and choose to avoid people in your routine who tempt you away from the things of God. Also, choose to avoid places that might tempt you, like ice cream shops with a gazillion flavors, or department stores with fashions you can't afford.

Choose Not to Worry

I hope and pray you are seeing worry for what it is—the choice of a bad habit that can and must be broken. Can't you just imagine a life without worry? Don't you desire the health and peace of body and mind that a worry-free life would bring?

And don't you yearn for burden-free days as you trust God, turning over every worry to Him and concentrating instead on trusting in His love and provision?

And don't you dream of possessing the energy you could have for focusing on serving others, the energy your fretting and anxiety is using up?

As you aim each day to choose not to worry, you can have all of the above—and more—and be completely free to serve God and those you love with all your heart and truly enjoy peace of mind. Look to God day by day, hour by hour, minute by minute, and choice by choice. He is ready, willing, and able to help you make this all-important choice to trust Him instead of worrying.

God's Guidelines for Making Right Choices... Choosing Not to Worry

These guidelines will help you proceed through your day, confident that you are seeking to make the right choices.

~ *Always choose to do what's right*—"To him who knows to do good and does not do it, to him it is sin" (James 4:17).

~ *Consult your Bible before making decisions*—"Your word is a lamp to my feet and a light to my path" (Psalm 119:105).

~ *Make no decision without prayer*—"Be anxious for nothing, but in everything by prayer and supplication, with thanksgiving, let your requests be made known to God" (Philippians 4:6).

~ *Seek counsel before making decisions*—"Without counsel, plans go awry, but in the multitude of counselors they are established" (Proverbs 15:22).

~ *Believe God has your best in mind*—"If you then, being evil, know how to give good gifts to your children, how much more will your Father who is in heaven give good things to those who ask Him!" (Matthew 7:11).

9

Managing Your Friendships

Walk with the wise and become wise; associate with fools and get in trouble.

—PROVERBS 13:20 NLT

Not too long ago my husband's cell phone finally gave out and we both were secretly glad for an opportunity to upgrade not only the phone, but also our calling plan. We must have had some sort of brain freeze when we chose the old phone's calling plan. You don't realize just how much you are talking on the phone until you get that monthly bill! It seemed that we had gone over our minutes on many occasions. I was always horrified, because even though many of those minutes were spent in ministering to people, many of them had also been spent talking to my friends—and I had the minute-count in front of me to prove exactly how many. I was shocked!

Well, needless to say, we made sure to sign up for a new plan with lots of minutes and nationwide service!

The Need for Friends

My friends are important to me, and I'm sure yours are too. And, my friend (for that's what I want to be to you), that's as it should be. You see, the Bible says you and I are created in the image of God (Genesis 1:26). That means we resemble God in some very special ways. And one of those ways is that, like God, we are social beings. That means...

We have fellowship with God. God created us to have fellowship with Himself, to be a friend. Now, God doesn't *need* us as friends, but He chooses to be our friend and to fellowship with us. And...

We can have friendship with Jesus Christ. God's Son, Jesus, has chosen for us to be His friends. Jesus declared:

> You are My friends if you do whatever I command you. No longer do I call you servants, for a servant does not know what his master is doing; but I have called you friends, for all things that I heard from My Father I have made known to you (John 15:14-15).

Understanding this very special relationship we can enjoy with God, and the friendship we can also have with Jesus, points to yet another choice we as God's women need to make—we need to choose our earthly friendships wisely. As daughters of the King and friends of Jesus Christ, our physical and human relationships are important. As children of God, we sit in places of honor. Therefore, improper or inappropriate friendships would dishonor our relationship with our heavenly Father and His Son, Jesus.

Immediately I'm thinking of several examples in the Bible of healthy friendships. One was between David and Jonathan in the

Old Testament. You can read their full story in 1 Samuel 18–20. It will take you a few minutes to read the details, but it will give you a good idea of how, even in spite of adversity, a friendship between peers grew in intense loyalty, constant encouragement, and lifelong commitment. Theirs was a friendship that was based on God and anchored in Him. As friends they encouraged each other to do what was right and just, and what was best for the other person.

Then we have the relationship between two women—Elizabeth, who was much older than Mary, who was a teenager (see Luke 1–2). Mary had been visited by the angel Gabriel and was pregnant by the Holy Spirit. So, she travels to see Elizabeth and get her advice. Elizabeth greets Mary as she enters into her home.

Then because they were both on the same godly path, they encouraged and assisted each other. They helped each other move forward through a difficult but exciting time. Both women were anticipating the delivery of two very unusual and very unique children—Jesus and John the Baptist.

Are you a woman who has never met a stranger? You can talk to others and make friends easily. Or maybe you have a long-time childhood or college friend, and the two of you are inseparable. But for a lot of women it's not easy to find a good friend, especially if you are like my two daughters, who move often.

So whether you have many friends or a few, I'm sure you will agree that friendship is a two-way street. If you want a good friend, you must be a good friend. So…

What Makes for a Good Friend?

In the Bible, God gives clear guidelines on how to be a friend, and how to choose a friend. As you read through these verses, ask yourself, *Am I a good friend?* Also, notice what a friend—a real friend—does and does not do.

He who covers a transgression seeks love, but he who repeats a matter separates friends (Proverbs 17:9).

A friend loves at all times, and a brother is born for adversity (Proverbs 17:17).

A man who has friends must himself be friendly, but there is a friend who sticks closer than a brother (Proverbs 18:24).

Faithful are the wounds of a friend, but the kisses of an enemy are deceitful (Proverbs 27:6).

Do not forsake your own friend (Proverbs 27:10).

As iron sharpens iron, so a man sharpens the countenance of a friend (Proverbs 27:17).

Being the Right Kind of Friend

You aren't responsible for what your friends do and don't do to you. But you *are* responsible for the kind of friend you are. Here are some choices you must make if you want to be a topnotch friend. When you make these choices, women—the right kind of women—will be knocking on your door wanting to be your friend!

Choose to grow closer to the Lord—If you desire to grow spiritually and know God more intimately, you will not settle for anything less than a friend who also shares your passion for God. You'll search high and low for a woman who's your twin in loving the Lord. And where will you find this kind of person who will share your passion for Jesus? Usually at church or in a women's Bible study or prayer group.

Choose to be yourself—There's no need to try to impress others by saying and doing things that aren't true of you. You are looking for a friend who isn't phony—so don't be phony yourself. If you are choosing to grow spiritually, then choose to be what God desires you to be—a godly woman. You may not be the most popular woman, but you will be what God wants you to be—genuine. Also, if you are comfortable with who you are, others will feel comfortable around you. Even if they don't have your beliefs, they will respect you for what you stand for. So just be yourself—your wonderful, sincere self. God will bring like-minded people to be your friends.

Choose to be loyal—not a fair-weather friend. I'm sure you know exactly what that means. It's a so-called friend who bails on you as soon as something bad happens. They are great friends as long as nothing gets complicated or sticky. Usually this type of friendship is one-way. As long as you do things their way or agree with them, everything is fine. But the minute you speak up or cross them or try being your own person, that "friend" fades away into the night. They want nothing to do with you.

Being loyal means being supportive, being ready to assist and encourage. That's why loyalty is so essential in any friendship. In the Bible, David and Jonathan's friendship was characterized by a solid loyalty even in the midst of adversity. They loved and encouraged each other in the Lord. They stood together through tough times like a set of identical stone bookends. They met as young men and warriors, and our last glimpse of their faithful friendship is of David mourning Jonathan's death. Theirs was a to-the-end-no-matter-what friendship. You can read about their friendship in 1 Samuel 20:14-17.

How does your loyalty rate as a friend? Are you "a friend who sticks closer than a brother" (Proverbs 18:24)? Loyalty in others starts with you being loyal.

Choose to be honest—Trust is another essential in any relationship. If you want to have friends who are honest with you, then you must be honest with them. Honesty is one of the benefits of a true friendship. The Bible puts it this way: "Wounds from a friend can be trusted…and the pleasantness of a friend springs from their heartfelt advice" (Proverbs 27:6,9 NIV). You and a true friend should be committed to pulling each other up toward God's goals and standards. Tell the truth. Keep your word. And speak up when something is not right. Oh, and remember: Honesty works both ways! Be willing to take advice and correction from a friend.

Choose to encourage—Have you ever thought about how easy it is to tell people all the things you think they are doing wrong? They are wearing the wrong clothes for the occasion or acting the wrong way. How much better it is to make a habit of picking out actions and attitudes that are right about others!

That's what David and Jonathan did. Their friendship was based on their mutual love for God. So when David was marked for murder by Jonathan's father, King Saul, Jonathan "arose and went to David…and strengthened his hand in God" (1 Samuel 23:16). Elizabeth and Mary also encouraged and blessed one another in the Lord.

God's message to us is to "encourage one another and build each other up" (1 Thessalonians 5:11 NIV). The best way to encourage a friend is to help them find strength in God. Share scriptures. Pray together. And give sincere compliments. Be specific with your praise. Point out things you appreciate about your friend, something you see in her conduct or admire in her character. Determine to build up others instead of tearing them down.

Choose to work at friendships—Good friendships, the right kind of friendships, don't just happen overnight. You have to make a willful choice about growing and keeping friendships. Like growing a garden, it takes time, care, effort, and prayer. It requires thought and planning—a phone call, an email, sitting with a friend who is ill or heartbroken, sharing a lunch, or just plain old spending some time together. I love what the apostle Paul said to his friends in Philippi: "I have you in my heart" (Philippians 1:7).

Do you have a best friend? What can you do today to nurture and cultivate that friendship?

Finding Friends

As a Christian, you already have a model relationship. You have a friend in Jesus Christ. God's Son, Jesus, has chosen you to be His friend. Just as with His disciples, Jesus speaks of you as His friend: "You are My friends...I have called you friends" (John 15:14-15). With Jesus as your friend, you really don't need anyone else.

But God also provides other people with whom you can and should have natural friendships. Women you meet at church are a natural starting point.

And what about making friends with your neighbors? Recently I spoke at a women's conference in California, and while I was there, I spent time visiting with a former next-door neighbor I hadn't seen in several decades. Amazingly, we picked up right where we had left off, before we both moved away those many years ago!

There are two other sources of friends that we often forget about. One is your parents. There is nothing weird about having your mom and dad as best friends. They are God's gift to you.

No one loves you more or cares for your best interests more than your parents. Make it a goal—and put in the time, effort, and money—to develop a deeper level of friendship with your parents. Work on it today and every day. And in later years you will be blessed and so glad you did.

Two, you also have friends in your brothers and sisters. As a child, you probably thought, *Friends with my goofy brother? No way!* or *Friends with my pesky little sister? You've got to be kidding!* But in truth, your friends throughout life come and go. You may stay in touch with some, but most of your friends will move on.

But your family is just that—your family. They will always be there, especially if you work at building and maintaining friendships with them. And that goofy brother of yours is all grown up and not so goofy anymore. And that pesky little sister is a woman with a family of her own. So pray for your family members, and your nieces and nephews! Make an effort to stay tight and close to your family.

God's List of People to Avoid

That doesn't sound very nice, does it? But the Bible is very clear and specific when it speaks to us about who to befriend… and who to avoid! Here's a short look at God's list of people to reject as friends. As you read through these verses, make a note about the speech, character, or conduct of those who are not to be your friends and the negative effects they can have on you.

> He who walks with wise men will be wise, but the companion of fools will be destroyed (Proverbs 13:20).

> Make no friendship with an angry man, and with a furious man do not go (Proverbs 22:24).

I have written to you not to keep company with anyone named a brother, who is sexually immoral, or covetous, or an idolater, or a reviler, or a drunkard, or an extortioner—not even to eat with such a person (1 Corinthians 5:11).

Do not be unequally yoked together with unbelievers. For what fellowship has righteousness with lawlessness? And what communion has light with darkness?…Or what part has a believer with an unbeliever? (2 Corinthians 6:14-15).

Do not be deceived: "Evil company corrupts good habits" (1 Corinthians 15:33).

Help! I'm in the Dating Stage

If this is you, remember to choose to go slow. Take your time. Guard your heart. And pray, pray, pray! Your goal is not merely a guy, but the right kind of guy. In the Bible you'll find a great model of the kind of guy you should be looking for and spending time with. Sometime soon take a few minutes and read the book of Ruth. (And don't worry—it's short!) See for yourself these qualities in Boaz:

- *Godly*—Look for a guy with a passion for Jesus. This should be #1 on your list. Boaz prayed to God to bless Ruth (Ruth 2:12).

- *Diligent*—Look for a guy who's a hard worker. Boaz was a careful manager of his property (2:1).

- *Friendly*—Look for a guy who will be your best friend. Boaz gave a warm greeting and welcomed Ruth to his field (2:4,8).

- *Merciful*—Look for a guy with compassion for others. Boaz asked about Ruth's situation and acted on her behalf (2:7).

- *Encouraging*—Look for a guy who contributes positively to your development. Boaz pointed out Ruth's strong qualities and spoke of them to encourage her (2:12).

- *Generous*—Look for a guy with a giving heart. Although Ruth needed food and worked for it, Boaz gave her extra (2:15).

- *Kind*—Look for a guy with a kind heart. The widow Naomi thanked God for Boaz's kindness toward her and Ruth (2:20).

- *Discreet*—Look for a guy who will protect your reputation. To avoid any speculation on her purity, Boaz sent Ruth home from the threshing floor before daylight (3:14).

- *Faithful*—Look for a guy who is true to his word. Boaz followed through on his promise to marry Ruth (4:1).[24]

Choosing a Godly Approach to Dating

Whether you call it dating or courting or just getting to know someone, finding the right potential guy is like navigating a maze! You're not exactly sure where you are going. But Boaz's example helps!

Boaz sounds like a great guy, doesn't he? Do you know anyone like him? Well, if not, be patient. He's out there, and God is working in him right now. In the meantime, here are some choices *you* need to be making as God prepares *you* for the right guy—the best man!

Choose to associate with men who are active, vibrant, for-real Christians. Develop a list of character qualities from the Bible that are a must for a Christian man you would want to date and possibly marry someday, if this is God's will. Then use that list as your guideline for the guys in your circle of friends today. Think about Boaz's godly traits. Look also at 1 Timothy 3 and Titus 1. There you'll see God praising men who are blameless in character and pure in conduct. That's the kind of guy you want to be praying for and spending time with. God desires the *best* for you, and you should too. Don't settle for anyone less than the best!

To put this even more strongly, *never* date someone who is not a Christian. The Bible is crystal clear on this. Second Corinthians 6:14 says, "Do not be yoked together with unbelievers. For what do righteousness and wickedness have in common? Or what fellowship can light have with darkness?" (NIV).

Here's how some popular youth and single adult leaders see this issue:

> Don't buy the "I can witness to him" myth. More often than not, when couples relate at different levels spiritually, the Christian is pulled away from God rather than the other way around.[25]

The writers go on to point out how a dating relationship with a non-Christian can only diminish who *you* are in Christ. There is no way dating an unbeliever can help your walk with Jesus grow stronger.

Choose to be patient as you watch and wait and pray for God to reveal His will. As you patiently wait, observe the single guys who are the spiritual leaders in your church and singles' group.

Note their character qualities. Listen to their conversation, what they talk about. Pay attention to how they treat others. And this may sound strong, but… do they read?

I've heard my husband give this advice to single women at every women's conference he has attended with me: "If a man doesn't read, he doesn't lead." A reader is a learner.

Choose to remain morally and sexually pure no matter what! Make this commitment to God and reaffirm it daily. His standard is absolute purity. This is a spiritual choice, and a wise choice, and a right choice. If a guy is godly and truly cares about you, then he will desire sexual purity for himself *and* for you. He will be all about encouraging your spiritual best, not tempting you to go against God's expressed will.

Dating at any age can take you on an emotional roller-coaster ride that hurts deeply when a relationship ends. Or affects your reputation. Or contributes negatively to your character development. Or gets you into sexual trouble and scars you for life. Don't let your emotions make your choices. So fix God's standards firmly in your heart and mind. Look to His Word—not your emotions—when you make your choices.

Three Kinds of People

There's no question that choosing friends and friendships is an important part of your life. Good, authentic friends are used by God to encourage, teach, support, and mature you. So choose them prayerfully and carefully.

I have observed that there are three kinds of people in life—

> those who pull you down,
> those who pull you along, and
> those who pull you up.

Obviously, you want to avoid those people who pull you down. "Bad company" does corrupt good character. So, this leaves only those who pull you along and pull you up as potential friends. Which means your best friends should be Christians—faithful-to-Christ friends who will pull you along and up toward Christlikeness. As you go about the business of looking for and choosing friends, be sure to...

Start with yourself. Nurture the qualities you desire in a friend. Be the kind of person who pulls others along and pulls them up toward the things of God.

And set the highest standards possible—those standards we've been discussing from the Bible. Remember, it's better to have no friends than to have the wrong friends!

Wow, what an important part of the many areas in which you must make choices—wouldn't you agree? Since this is such an important area, I can't resist with this final word of review as your friend:

A good friend should be a strong, like-minded Christian who will help you to think your best thoughts, do your most honorable deeds, and be your finest self. As always, who you choose as a friend is your choice. Choose wisely!

God's Guidelines for Making Right Choices...Choosing Friends

These guidelines will help you proceed through your day, confident that you are seeking to make the right choices.

~ *Choose friends who will be loyal.* "One who has unreliable friends soon comes to ruin, but there is a friend who sticks closer than a brother" (Proverbs 18:24 NIV).

~ *Choose friends who will be faithful.* "A friend loves at all times, and a brother is born for adversity" (Proverbs 17:17).

~ *Choose friends who will hold you accountable.* "As iron sharpens iron, so a man sharpens the countenance of his friend" (Proverbs 27:17).

~ *Choose friends who will encourage your growth.* "My dear friends, as you have always obeyed, not as in my presence only, but now much more in my absence—work out your own salvation with fear and trembling" (Philippians 2:12).

~ *Choose friends who will pray for you.* "For this reason, since the day we heard about you, we have not stopped praying for you. We continually ask God to fill you with the knowledge of his will through all the spiritual wisdom and understanding that the Spirit gives" (Colossians 1:9 NIV).

10

Keeping Watch over What You Say

Let the words of my mouth...
be acceptable in Your sight, O LORD.
—PSALM 19:14

*I*t happened again! Even after I had *promised* myself that I wouldn't do it again. And what's worse, I had also promised God.

But there I was, standing in the church parking lot, of all places, totally dejected! The circle of ladies that had surrounded me had made their about-faces and quickly moved off to their respective cars. Each one was relishing the information I had so quickly and thoughtlessly divulged. Each one was savoring the "dainty morsels" (as Proverbs 18:8 NASB calls them) I had fed them.

Yes, this band of sisters had received their weekly injection of gossip! Now they were on their way to spread the latest tidings to their own network of eager recipients of the latest news and dirt. Never mind what this news might do to reputations and relationships!

Sounds pretty bad when I describe it this way, doesn't it? There was a time when I didn't think anything about it. It was something we all did. There was always "the meeting after the meeting." And we were all equally guilty of the same sin. Actually, at the time I didn't see what we were doing as "sin." I don't think I would have intentionally sinned. Yet that was exactly what I was doing. I was choosing to gossip!

I was speaking on a variation of this story at my daughter's church in New York, and she (Katherine) came up to me during the break and said, "Mom, you need to finish the story. What you shared sounds like this just happened yesterday instead of 20 years ago!" So after the break, I "finished the story"—I explained how God had convicted my heart and brought about change in my life.

And praise God, I'm not the same person today. And praise Him again, the words pouring out of my mouth are not the words they once were. By God's grace I've experienced victory and transformation in this one vital area of right choices—my mouth! Oh, I still slip up once in a great while, but gossip is not a part of my daily habit.

So how did I gain victory? How did I master my mouth? Read on!

Learning About Gossip

Let's start this section off with a little quiz:

Can You Guess Who I Am?

I ruin without killing. I tear down homes. I break hearts and wreck lives. You will find me in the pews of the pious as well as in the haunts of the unholy.

I gather strength with age. I have made my way where greed, distrust, and dishonor are unknown; yet my victims are as numerous as the sands of the sea, and often as innocent. *My name is Gossip.*[26]

It's a horrible fact: Everyone has been hurt by gossip. No one is immune from the searing pain brought about by false or damaging information. I know I've been on the receiving end of such pain and damage. And I'm ashamed to say I've been the deliverer of it too. You've probably experienced both ends of gossip as well.

Oh dear! Can you hear me groaning? That's because merely *thinking* about gossip—or saying the word—brings back some really sickening memories of my blunders in this area. In a moment I'll get to more about how I overcame this terrible habit. For now, let me say that I first started knowing victory when I learned about the meaning of the word *gossip*.

Upon hearing it, the word *gossip* doesn't sound so awful, does it? I researched this word in my dictionary, and it defined gossip as a casual conversation about other people. That doesn't sound so bad, does it?

And in the past, there was a sense in which gossip had a role in society. News was shared verbally. Ladies of good reputation did not go out on the streets or to the market by themselves. Therefore, they relied on news from others. Maids and servants gathered the latest tidings and information on people and events from both near and far. Then that news was passed on.

The reason I refer to the habit of gossiping as a killer, then, is because of what I found out after doing further research. I was shocked to discover that to gossip literally means "to throw down, bring down, or throw through." Think about it: What does a gossip or a slanderer do? Kill people. Oh, not in the literal sense. But by passing on negative information about a person, a gossip brings down that person's reputation. She throws down that person's good name. Through mere words, a slanderer kills the reputation that some poor unsuspecting victim has worked so hard all her life to build.

Other definitions for *gossip* include "idle talker" and "tattler." And, if you're honest, you know that most gossip occurs when you *aren't* doing something useful. You talk on the phone with a best friend, sister, or close acquaintance—and before you know it, you are talking negatively about another person! Or, like me, you pass time in the church parking lot waiting for church to start, or having that "meeting" after church.

It takes only two for gossip to happen. And when two women get together, talking occurs naturally. Which makes it very easy for gossip to happen as well!

The Bible's Take on Gossip

The Bible aims some very sharp arrows of warning and instruction directly at women about their mouths. In doing so it refers to them as gossips, slanderers, and malicious slanderers. Ho hum—this is nothing new or earth-shattering.

Then we get down to a few choice definitions. A *slanderer* is defined as one who makes a false or damaging statement about another person's reputation. Now that's a pretty serious issue, isn't it? Enter "the killer"—also known as gossip!

Did you know the Bible contains a list of qualities God desires in Christian women of all ages? In Titus 2:4, we read that the older women are to "admonish the young women" in what they themselves have learned. One of those life-lessons is teaching other women "not [to be] slanderers" (Titus 2:3). This means gossip and slander are *not* godly qualities and are therefore out—or off limits—for you and me as Christians. For sure it's hard not to gossip. But it's even more sobering to know that gossip is to have no place or part in our lives. That's *no* as in *zero!*

Recently, while recording some radio broadcasts, it finally happened—the topic of gossip came up. That meant I was forced to share this sickening information:

> The word *slanderer* is used many times in the Bible. And it has a frightening meaning! Slanderer comes from the word *diabolos*, meaning a malicious gossip, slanderer, or false accuser. This word is used 34 times (yes, 34!) in the New Testament as a title for Satan. It is also used to describe Judas, the disciple who betrayed Jesus and was called "a devil" in John 6:70. And, besides these references, the word is used in Titus 2:3 and in 1 Timothy 3:11 in reference to women, literally meaning "she-devils" and "malicious talkers."

Gossips are not in very good company, are they? They are lumped together with Satan, Judas, and slanderous "she-devil" women—not a pretty or pleasant thought, is it? Even the most hardened offender (gulp!) might be ashamed of her gossiping if she realized she was a she-devil involved in slandering and killing others.

Learning from Others

Sadly, the Bible shows us many females who participated in the destruction of others through ungodly and unchecked gossip. Here are a few examples:

Potiphar's wife. You can read the full story of how this woman tempted Joseph in Genesis 39, but here's how Potiphar's wife lied to her husband and falsely accused the righteous Joseph: "Now Joseph was handsome in form and appearance. And it came to pass after these things that his master's wife cast longing eyes on Joseph, and she said, 'Lie with me.' But he refused…then she spoke to [her husband telling him a false story]…Then Joseph's master took him and put him into the prison" (verses 6-8,17,20).

What was the outcome of this woman's malicious and slanderous report? God's servant Joseph spent about three years in prison (Genesis 40).

Jezebel set into motion the false accusation that the righteous Naboth had blasphemed God and her husband, the king—all because Naboth wouldn't sell his field to the king. She conspired with the leaders of the city to slander Naboth. "Two men, scoundrels, came in and sat before him; and the scoundrels witnessed against him, against Naboth, in the presence of the people, saying, 'Naboth has blasphemed God and the king!'"

The result? "Then they took him outside the city and stoned him with stones, so that he died" (1 Kings 21:13).

Martha maligned both her sister and the Lord. She both defamed and attacked their character. Upset that Mary wasn't helping her with preparations for a large number of guests, Martha exclaimed, "Lord, do You not care that my sister has left me to serve alone? Therefore tell her to help me" (Luke 10:40).

The result? Martha was rebuked and corrected by Jesus. And Mary, who had chosen to stop her busy service and listen to the Lord, was praised by Him.

These are very obvious examples of the consequences that result when we choose to open our mouths in a sinful manner, aren't they? But gossip is a practice and a choice that has many disguises. Maybe this picture of three different types of gossip will shed some further light on any misconceptions you might have about gossip.

Three Categories of Gossip

Malicious gossip. Malicious gossip is consciously and deliberately hurtful. It is based in envy and rooted in flagrant selfishness. It is designed to break up relationships and destroy friendships. And it can manifest itself in all kinds of evil deeds.

Rationalization. Rationalization is far more subtle than malicious gossip. What makes rationalization so dangerous is that it often results from self-deception. Rooted and based in the same motives as malicious gossip, the person who has rationalized has convinced herself that she is doing it for "the good" of the other person. She may disguise it as "prayer interest" and "personal concern." Nevertheless, rationalization is very destructive.

Innocent gossip. This involves a person who truly is concerned, but who is, to a certain extent, unwise and insensitive to other people's feelings. Innocent gossip is sometimes motivated by a desire to be "helpful," but in reality the gossiper may be trying to prove to others "how helpful she really is." In this situation there is a very fine line between selfish and unselfish motives. All Christians must beware of this kind of gossip.[27]

Aiming for Godly Speech

Hallelujah—at last I got it! I thank God that His message to me was finally glaring and blaring: My habit of ungodly speech and—more specifically, gossip—had to be dealt with.

So, here's what I learned about what it means to have godly speech. Obviously godly speech goes way beyond dealing with and eliminating gossip. It also includes choosing not to lie, curse, tell dirty jokes, or use what the Bible refers to as suggestive or "filthy language" (Colossians 3:8). And of course the Bible shines the spotlight on gossip and we want to do the same in this chapter because it seems so harmless. After all, when you listen to what people are saying, it seems like "everyone is doing it"— and therefore, it's okay.

Dear friend, I hope you are as struck by these awful definitions and illustrations as I am. Gossip always has an effect! And I hope you desire to follow God's calling to godly speech too.

In the past, I failed miserably in the area of gossip. But then I learned the truth about gossip, the ugly facts we've been looking at. It was then that I began to purpose—every day when I woke up—to live out God's command to put away all malice and evil speaking (Ephesians 4:31). It's been life-changing! It hasn't been—and still isn't—easy. Opportunities to gossip abound. But I'm committed to making the effort day by day to refrain from engaging in gossip.

To help you (and remind me!), I began to ask and answer the following questions that aim for godly speech.

How can I avoid gossiping?

Put these tactics to work for you. Take it from me—they work!

To begin, *think the best about others.* Refuse to think the worst of them. Instead, train yourself to assume the best in their words and actions. Apply these guidelines from Philippians 4:8 to what you hear about people: "Whatever things are true...noble... just...pure...lovely...of good report, if there is any virtue and if there is anything praiseworthy—meditate on these things."

Next, *agree with your friends not to gossip.* Share with those closest to you about your desire to grow in this area. Tell them about your goal and the changes you want to make, and why. And ask them to let you know when you've slipped up and gossiped.

Also, *avoid settings that can lead to gossip.* Well, at least be on the alert for them. You probably already know the list—luncheons, parties, showers, and even church meetings. Instead, make it a goal to be with groups of women in a Bible study or in a discipleship setting where the aim is spiritual growth and exposure to God's Word and His truths.

It goes without saying—*avoid women who gossip.* You'll find that, unfortunately, there are certain women who gossip regularly and are even skillful at drawing others—including you—into it.

Try to *say nothing.* If your mouth is closed, it's hard to gossip. Have you ever heard the quip, "It's better to be thought a fool than to open your mouth and prove it"? Well, say nothing! You'll be way ahead.

How can I work at eliminating gossip from my life?

Here are three T's you might find helpful. I try to abide by them every day:

> *Telephone*—Beware of endless chatting on the phone! Let your voice mail or answering machine handle your calls. Then when you talk on the phone, preface your calls with something like, "I have only a few minutes."
>
> And don't forget to email and text. You'll be tempted to say a lot less. Plus you have the harsh benefit of seeing

your words in print or on a screen! When you see that
your words are not pretty, you can change what you say,
or just not say it at all.

Talk—I should say, "Talk less." But when you do talk, or
if you must talk, don't talk too long. As the proverb
teaches us, "In the multitude of words sin is not lacking,
but he who restrains his lips is wise" (Proverbs 10:19).
Be wise. Talk less.

Tarry—Don't be quick to respond to what people are talking
about. Wait to give input or opinions. You don't have
to quickly answer every question you're asked. Sometimes quick answers can get you into lots of trouble!
You have every right to ask for time to think and pray
about things before (and if) you answer. A hasty answer
is usually a foolish answer. "Do you see a man hasty in
his words? There is more hope for a fool than for him"
(Proverbs 29:20).

How can I make permanent changes in my speech?

Remember these basic truths and tactics.

Remember the source of slander—This, of course, is the devil.
Once you recall this before you open your mouth, you'll
probably close it right away!

Realize the cause of slander—Among the causes are hatred,
jealousy, envy, and an evil heart. Not a very pretty list,
is it? Instead your aim should be "sweet speech."

Choose your company carefully—Isolate yourself, if you
must, until you get it right. That's what I did. I took
a "word fast" during which I said nothing until I could

say something good. Then, when you do choose your company, choose women who have only positive things to say about others.

Choose your activities carefully—Be careful about talking on the phone, hanging out, or staying too long after your luncheon appointment with your friends is over.

Choose words of praise—Be known as a woman who is a friend of women. I call this being a woman who is *for* other women rather than being *against* them. God wants you to share words that are full of grace (Colossians 4:6), wise and kind (Proverbs 16:23-24; 31:26), pleasant, sweet, constructive, and instructive. May your speech edify and minister grace to your hearers (Ephesians 4:29).

Choose to pray—Rather than talk about someone who has issues, pray for them. And while you're at it, pray for yourself and your speech. Also pray for those who harm you. This way, you're telling the right person—God, not everyone else—about your problems. His job is to deal with those who wrong you (Romans 12:19). Your job is to pray and to forgive.

Choose to deal with gossip as sin—This is where I had my greatest breakthrough. Acknowledge to God that you have a problem with gossip. Confess it as sin. Tell Him all about it (1 John 1:8-9). And ask for His help.

What should I do when others gossip?

So let's imagine you are making headway with your problem. Now what are you supposed to do when you're among other women who gossip? It's good to be prepared, and these options will help.

Choose to leave the scene. When gossip surfaces at your next gathering, follow Joseph's example when he found himself in a compromising situation—he fled (Genesis 39:12). In the New Testament, Paul told the young pastor Timothy to flee from temptation (2 Timothy 2:22). So flee! Leave the room. Get out. ASAP. Excuse yourself. Go get a breath of fresh air. Make a phone call. Powder your nose. Shoot up a prayer to God. Ask Him for His wisdom about the best way to handle the situation.

Choose to speak up and declare your discomfort. I learned a valuable lesson in a Bible study one morning when the teacher stopped the lesson and announced, "I'm sorry. Maybe it's just me, but I'm not comfortable with this conversation. Could we please change the subject or move on with our lesson?"

Also, when I hear someone say, "Don't tell anyone, but..." I raise my hands and interrupt with, "Well, then don't tell me!"

Choose to be ready with a positive phrase or two. I like to come to the aid of the one being maligned. For instance, I'll say, "Oh, no—bless her heart!" Or "Oh, that just couldn't be true! She's too kind to do something like that."

Choose to use your tongue to glorify God—After all, the tongue was created to glorify the Lord. To gossip and slander is to pervert its use for that which is ungodly.

You may or may not know that I have written a number of tween and teen girl books, and as I was doing my research I came across this heart-wrenching testimonial from a girl. I think you will agree that she had some great insights that could be useful to most, if not all, women of any age!

Regrettable Words

I've said some things in my life that I've regretted. One of the biggest things I regret saying involves a girl I hardly knew. When I was with a bunch of my friends at a slumber party, I started gossiping about this girl—talking about her behind her back and saying things about her that just weren't true. Eventually she found out, and I lost the chance to ever be her friend. I tried to make things right, but she never said another word to me.

It was low of me to try to impress my friends by gossiping about an innocent person. Proverbs 3:29 says that I should not do any harm to the people around me. When I gossiped about this girl, I hurt her, and I hurt God too. God created each person in a special way. When we make fun of someone, it's like we're telling God, "That girl or guy isn't good enough for me." And how can we do that when that person is good enough for God?

—Megan[28]

Choosing to Monitor Your Mouth

One of the most frequent important choices you must make is the choice to monitor your mouth. The best solution is to say nothing. But, if you must speak, then make the choice to control your tongue. The Bible has high praise for anyone who controls their speech. It says you will be "a perfect [woman], able to bridle [your] whole body" (James 3:2). What a great goal to aspire to! And, as in everything, the choice is yours. You can slander others, or you can love them.

If you develop a heart of love—love for the Lord, love for His Word, love for His people, love for others—then you won't gossip. Gossip and slander pervert your mouth from what it was created for—to glorify God. I urge you, start now. Stay true. Shine brilliantly as one who speaks words of truth and kindness. If you do this, you will truly be an exceptional woman all the days of your life.

God's Guidelines for
Making Right Choices...
Choosing Your Words Carefully

These guidelines will help you proceed through your day, confident that you are seeking to make the right choices.

~ *Control your emotions*—"Whoever has no rule over his own spirit is like a city broken down, without walls" (Proverbs 25:28).

~ *Control your life by controlling your mouth*— "Whoever guards his mouth and tongue keeps his soul from troubles" (Proverbs 21:23).

~ *Confine your mouth to good uses*—"Let no corrupt word proceed out of your mouth, but what is good for necessary edification, that it may impart grace to the hearers" (Ephesians 4:29).

~ *Commit your mouth to God*—"Let the words of my mouth and the meditation of my heart be acceptable in Your sight, O LORD, my strength and my Redeemer" (Psalm 19:14).

~ *Consider that your mouth can do great damage*— "Even so the tongue is a little member and boasts great things. See how great a forest a little fire kindles!" (James 3:5).

11

Expanding Your Mind

Give instruction to a wise man, and he
will be still wiser; teach a just man, and he
will increase in learning.
—Proverbs 9:9

According to those who keep track of statistics, those who were born in the 1980s or later—and that might include you!—have experienced a time of unusually great prosperity and opportunity. But not too many years ago, prospects weren't so bright.

Let me tell you about my precious mother-in-law, Lois. Jim's mom was raised in a period of time referred to as the Great Depression. Jobs were few and far between. If a person was lucky enough to have a job, the pay was usually meager—not even enough to provide for the barest essentials for a family. If you wanted to go to a local restaurant for a full Thanksgiving dinner, complete with dessert and beverage, it would have cost you about $1.25. We don't view the price of that dinner as very high, but more than half of the families in America didn't have $1.25 to spare for such a meal! Today you can't even buy a cup of coffee for this price!

Lois grew up in a tiny mining town in Oklahoma. As one of the older girls in her family, she had to help support the family. As a result, she wasn't able to finish high school, completing only grades 1 through 8. But that didn't keep her from wanting to learn and grow intellectually. She became an avid reader and years later, finished her GED (General Education Development diploma). Even later, while in her forties, she went back to school and became an LVN (Licensed Vocational Nurse).

And here's where you and I can take lessons in learning and growing. As Lois grew older, rather than moving more toward a lighter fare intellectually, she increasingly read more and more of her Bible. She also devoured audio Bible-preaching messages. She couldn't be at church enough to soak in her pastor's expounding of God's Word. Plus, she read Christian books with a voracious hunger. As the years passed, Lois read books on topics that were steadily heavier content-wise—book on theology, treatises on the nature of God, and whole commentaries on the books of the Bible.

So you can see the example that she has left behind for me and my family after she went to be with the Lord. I can still recall going into her bedroom after her death and seeing the stack of books on her nightstand. Most had been read, while others were waiting for her eager mind and heart.

A Dose of Reality

Thinking of Lois and her desire to learn reminds me of the story of how the young men and women of my husband's small hometown struggled with the question of whether continuing one's education and learning was important or not. The town Jim grew up in had a large manufacturing plant that hired many of the local residents. Every year a large number of the high school graduates would achieve their life goal of going to work for the plant or for a local business that was in some way connected with the plant. When Jim's friends finished high school, most of them counted on getting jobs in the local area. They were good-paying jobs, but they didn't require more than a basic high school education.

Jim too was heading in that direction—just going through the motions at school, not really that interested in an education, until a local pharmacist took an interest in him and hired him to work in his pharmacy. Over a period of time Jim's focus turned from eventually working at the local plant to getting the training to become a pharmacist.

The sad part of this story is that the local plant closed the year after Jim graduated from high school! Many of his high-school friends, as well as about half the town, lost their jobs and income. And because most of the workers and young people had not planned ahead and at least made an effort to do well in school, their prospects for their future at the tire plant were dashed on the rocks of reality.

She Died Learning

Are you beginning to see where I'm heading in this chapter? Well, if you have yet to guess, maybe these words that were chiseled on the tombstone of a well-known scientist might help: "He Died Learning." Every time I read this epitaph, it continues to make a great impression on me.

Through the years, I've tried to follow this man's example. I want those I know to say of me, "She died learning." And, my friend, I hope this will become your motto as well because I don't want something like Jim's small-town experience to happen to you.

Unfortunately, life takes unexpected turns, and if you're not prepared, you can find yourself in a difficult place. You may wake up tomorrow only to discover that your dream of going into a specific career or your goal of being a stay-at-home-mom is no longer possible. Or you may realize that you are now responsible for your own support. Or you and your husband are beginning to consider homeschooling your children. And guess who is sure to be elected as their teacher? (Eek!)

So commit yourself to being a lifetime learner. Formal learning takes place with textbooks and, in most cases, within the four walls of a classroom. But there is also informal learning. This type of learning isn't dependent on ability as much as on your personal interests, needs, and desires. You get to choose what you want to learn, and the choices are limitless! All you have to do is fit it into your day. It's an ongoing activity that should last your entire lifetime.

For instance, I just had lunch with a young single woman after church on Sunday who is one month away from receiving her bachelor's degree in event planning and coordination from an online university. For the past five years she has worked part-time, served in her church as director of the children, youth, and young adult ministries, and kept on learning as she's inched her way toward a college degree.

And here's another kind of learning. After the surgical removal of a malignant cancerous growth, one of my daughters "went back to school," so to speak. Married with an active, busy family, she chose to spend odd moments of time daily—and nightly—researching dietary information and health recommendations for her condition. Today she is a walking encyclopedia on health, fitness, food, and vitamins. God has greatly used her to share His love and grace with others who seek her out as she gives out the treasure of the educational information she has gleaned from her personal quest for knowledge.

And then, of course, there is the example of the fully mature Lois, my mom-in-law. And I'm also thinking of Debbie, my sweet sister-in-law, who went back to school to get a law degree when her children left for college.

All of these wonderful women desired to learn and somehow worked it into their busy lives and around family responsibilities. Now, where do you fit? And what are you dreaming of doing? And what are you doing to grow today?

Learning as a Lifestyle

For several decades I enjoyed a mentoring ministry to women at my kitchen table. What a blessing to spend time each week with "girl talk" and have the opportunity to get to know these awesome sisters in Christ and pour my life into theirs!

But I have to tell you, one of the conditions I set for our meetings was that they commit to reading every day. Number one on the list of books to read (as I'm sure you can guess) was the Bible. Beyond that, if a woman was married, she was to select, purchase, borrow, or check out a book on marriage and read five minutes a day in that book. If she was a mom (you guessed this too), she was to select, purchase, borrow, or check out a book on raising children and read five minutes a day in that book. And yes, I really did this—because every woman lives somewhere, she was to select, purchase, borrow, or check out a book on home management and read five minutes a day in that book. Beyond that, all my gals were to choose an area where they desired to grow as a Christian (like prayer, self-discipline, worship) and—you got it!—select, purchase, borrow, or check out a book on their topic and read five minutes a day in that book.

My goals for these ladies? First of all, to ground them in the faith. And second, to help them be on their toes with fresh input and reminders through their reading for tending their priority relationships and roles. And for all, married or not, to be growing as a Christian and preparing for future ministry…just by learning something each day they could pass on to others. All this—accomplished in only minutes a day!

I told each one of my disciples about Ruth Graham, wife of the famed evangelist Billy Graham, and what she told her daughters: "Keep reading and you'll be educated."[29] The same applies to you, dear friend and reader!

Now take a look at these concepts about learning:

Learning is an attitude—it involves heart and head.

Learning is cumulative—it builds upon itself.

Learning is not dependent on your IQ—it is all about your DQ, or your desire quotient.

Learning has no boundaries—except those you place on yourself.

Learning does not require social status or money—it's free to anyone who desires to grow in knowledge.

Learning has its own rewards—its prizes are limitless.

Learning has an ultimate priority—knowing more about Jesus Christ (Philippians 3:10; 2 Peter 3:18).

God's Perspective on Learning

I sure hope you are becoming convinced about the importance of continuing to learn and train yourself for wise living and for serving God. God created you and me with an incredible resource called a brain. This fascinating organ is more complex than any computer. And God expects us to put it to good use. As you look over these verses, think about how they point out

the necessity of learning. And don't forget to notice the blessings God showers on those who "increase learning."

> Hear, my children, the instruction of a father, and
> give attention to know understanding; for I give
> you good doctrine: Do not forsake my law (Prov-
> erbs 4:1-2).

> Get wisdom! Get understanding! Do not forget,
> nor turn away from the words of my mouth. Do
> not forsake her, and she will preserve you; love
> her, and she will keep you. Wisdom is the prin-
> cipal thing; therefore get wisdom. And in all your
> getting, get understanding. Exalt her, and she will
> promote you; she will bring you honor, when you
> embrace her. She will place on your head an orna-
> ment of grace; a crown of glory she will deliver to
> you (Proverbs 4:5-9).

> A wise man will hear and increase learning, and
> a man of understanding will attain wise counsel
> (Proverbs 1:5).

How to Enjoy a Life of Learning

I'm sure you know others who, like Lois, chose to enroll in a
school or university for several years to earn a degree. They paid
money for tuition and books, submitted themselves to a curric-
ulum and faculty, did the work of taking exams and writing
papers. These students had a goal and they went for it. Bravo!

But you too, my dear friend, can grow right where you are,
no matter what. Your growth can be daily and natural—even
easy. And here are a few simple choices for continuing to learn
for a lifetime:

Choose to be a zealous reader. Reading is the window to all learning. Reading exposes you to the entire globe and to the knowledge and experiences of others. Say, for instance, you read one of my books, like this one! The information you read in a few hours or days took me many years—even decades—to formulate. But in a very short time, you can know most of what I know on the subject of making choices. How's that for learning from others?

You have only so much time, so be selective in your reading. Choose books that will build you up—books that will encourage and inspire you! Books that will teach and train you. Don't forget—the first book you want to read and read again and again is the Bible. Read it a little at a time from cover to cover, over and over, for the rest of your life. It is the book that will help as you face cancer or deal with difficult problems with your husband or children. The Bible—often referred to as "the Book"—will help you through the storms of life.

Choose to ask questions. Everyone is an expert on something and has something to teach you. Find out what that something is, and learn from these people. Approach every person as your teacher. Is there someone who is doing something you would like to learn about? Do you like to cook? Who can expand your abilities in this area? Are you thinking of homeschooling? Who can you meet with to find out more about what's involved? Want to find out how to study the Bible? Ask someone who's passionate about it.

Choose to observe the lives of others. Look around you for models you can follow—or basket cases to avoid! Who at church is doing things you would like to learn how to do? How about in your neighborhood, or your workplace? Who seems to have their act together? Who seems to be a mess? Who seems to be living a godly life, moving in the direction you want to go? Observe both the good and bad. Take note of both. Then copy the good actions of others, and avoid the bad.

Choose to learn from the experiences of others. It's been noted that the person who is limited to depending upon his or her own past experiences has relatively little material to work with. Say, for instance, you want to be a writer. Where should you start? Find someone who has written a book or has published articles in magazines. Ask her how she got started and what advice she can give you.

The same goes for your questions about missionary work, or the medicine field. Just ask someone with experience. It's never too late to learn.

Also, you can learn incredible life lessons from the biographies of the great men and women of history. Whenever I'm asked what kinds of books I like to read, the answer is always "Biographies!" I learn so much from others' experiences as leaders, wives, and moms. I soak up their faith experiences with sorrow, loss, prayer, suffering...and great victories and triumphs. Reading is a quick way to learn from people's successes as well as from their mistakes.

And I have to say it again—don't forget your Bible. The Bible is the best of all books for learning from the experiences of others.

Choose to stretch yourself. You may be at a point in your life when you are somewhat comfortable with everything you are doing. This isn't a bad thing. But if staying on cruise control describes your present attitude, and you have no interest whatsoever in stretching yourself, maybe a quote my husband gave me might persuade you to have second thoughts about this kind of attitude.

One of Jim's hobbies (like mine) is reading biographies of military leaders. One of his favorite generals of World War II is Douglas MacArthur. This is what MacArthur said about life and learning:

> Life is a lively process of becoming. If you haven't added to your interests during the past year, if you are thinking the same thoughts, relating the same personal experiences, having the same predictable reactions—rigor mortis of the personality has set in.[30]

I'm sure you want nothing to do with rigor mortis, the temporary stiffness that occurs in your muscles when you die. So learning is living. You're not dead, so make sure you aren't acting like it. That's my prayer for both of us.

The Importance of Today

Now don't get the wrong idea. I'm not encouraging you to go back to school, or spend an excessive amount of time buried in a bunch of books or slumped in front of a computer monitor. Maybe you've already been there and done that.

What I am encouraging you to consider is the importance of learning…just for today. The habits and disciplines you acquire daily will lay the foundation for the rest of your life, no matter what your age. Today, you are as young as you will ever be, so today is a good day to learn. You can choose today—and every day—to grow in your knowledge of the things of God and in areas that stimulate you to keep moving forward in a life of learning…and living.

Take advantage of today—and every day—to learn and grow. And that begins by choosing not to waste today. Think about these truths about the choices you make today:

Today's *good decisions* will give you the freedom to choose greater opportunities tomorrow.

Today's *good habits* will give you greater discipline for choosing to accept greater challenges tomorrow.

Today's *good attitudes* will equip you to choose to run the greater race and for winning the greater prize tomorrow (1 Corinthians 9:24).

Choosing to Learn

I have what I call a "sticky note habit." I can't help myself. Every store I shop in, I look at the sticky notes. In my office supply cupboard you'll find them in every color, size, and shape. And I use them—on my computer, my planner, my refrigerator, and my microwave door. They're even on my bathroom mirror so I see them first thing each morning. Well, here are four questions you can put on a sticky note on your mirror—and everywhere else. Happy learning!

- What new thing can I learn *today*?
- Who can I learn from *today*?
- How can I be stretched in some aspect of my life *today*?
- How can I become more Christlike *today*?

God's Guidelines for Making Right Choices... Choosing to Learn

These guidelines will help you proceed through your day, confident that you are seeking to make the right choices.

~ *Follow in Jesus' footsteps*—"Jesus increased in wisdom and stature, and in favor with God and men" (Luke 2:52).

~ *Focus on God*—"Seek first the kingdom of God and His righteousness, and all these things shall be added to you" (Matthew 6:33).

~ *Apply yourself*—"Be diligent to present yourself approved to God, a worker who does not need to be ashamed, rightly dividing the word of truth" (2 Timothy 2:15).

~ *Give your all*—"Whatever your hand finds to do, do it with your might" (Ecclesiastes 9:10).

~ *Respond to God's challenge*—"Grow in the grace and knowledge of our Lord and Savior Jesus Christ" (2 Peter 3:18).

12

$\mathcal{P}$racticing $\mathcal{Y}$our $\mathcal{P}$riorities,

Part 1

*I press toward the goal for the prize
of the upward call of God in Christ Jesus.*
—PHILIPPIANS 3:14

August 31, 1974, was a red-letter day in my life. Wow! That was the day Jim and I sat down together and made a decision to each write some lifetime goals. Up until that day, I had flopped and floundered and made little or no progress in achieving much of anything with lasting godly influence. Basically I had spent the first 28 years of my life as an unbeliever, drifting from one desire to another—and for sure without God in mind! Oh, there was always a nagging feeling or emptiness somewhere in the recesses of my heart that there must be more to life than what I was experiencing. And praise God, there was! I met Jesus at age 28 and was born again, with open eyes and an open heart ready to serve God. I'd had enough of doing things my way. It wasn't too long before Jim and I sat down at our dining room table to start an exercise that would transform us forever.

On that life-changing Sunday afternoon, we prayed and asked God to give us wisdom as we sat down to write our goals—goals that I hoped would line up my life with God's will. Jim sat beside me, and shoulder to shoulder, we went through this exercise together.

Today, both Jim and I are still operating our lives according to those goals that were written with hearts full of hope—goals that have helped to simplify our choices in life, goals that have allowed me to be a support to my husband and an influence on my children, goals that have enabled me to also have an impact on women in my church and outside my church as well.

Why are goals such an important part of making right choices? Or maybe a better way to say it is, Why are they a vital part of helping me to make the *best* choices in life? Because goals help you to define your purpose. As a child of God you don't want to miss out on even the smallest part of God's will and purpose for you.

It's true that the poorest of all people is not the one without *gold*, but the one without *goals*. I know from my own experience that life for a goalless woman has no significant meaning or purpose. And without goals, not only do we lack direction, but we also lack impact! By contrast, goals give you direction, purpose, and help you know how to best use your time and energy—thus making you a woman of impact.

Eight Areas of Life that Call for Goals

It's been said, "If you don't know where you are going, then any road will get you there." Or put another way, "If you don't have a clue about your life, then any old choice will do." Sure, you will make choices. But will they be the right ones? Who knows? Without direction for your life, you won't even know whether or not you are on the right path until it is probably too late. You could make the worst possible choice for your life, but without goals to guide you, you'll have no idea whether your choices are moving you forward…or backward. And because choices have consequences, you may end up with results that make your life worse rather than better.

But life doesn't have to be that way. You don't have to blunder your way through it. When you set goals based on God's priorities, you will be able to determine the choices to make. Let's start with eight areas of life that are key priorities for your time and attention.

Spiritual—Your spiritual health is the key—the secret—to being a woman who makes right choices. Spiritual maturity is the starting point for all of your life, including making the best possible choices. What's more, you cannot impart to others what you do not possess yourself. And the thing that is most important to impart to others is your vibrant, growing life in Christ.

You and I must also realize that spiritual growth is not optional. In fact, we are commanded in Scripture to grow in grace and knowledge (2 Peter 3:18). Spiritual exercise, like physical exercise, must be continuous to remain healthy. So consider stepping up your efforts. You can never live on past spirituality.

Here are some choices you can make to "exercise" yourself to achieve greater spiritual growth:

> —Make sure your Bible is handy. Read it every day… and take it everywhere you go.
>
> —The Bible says you are to pray frequently, fervently, constantly, continuously, without ceasing, and about any and every thing. So…pray!

—Attending church is essential. Don't give up your search until you find one that promotes your spiritual growth.

—Mature Christians can help you grow. Seek out a woman who can serve as a mentor.

If you worry that you don't have the time to focus on these spiritual disciplines, please don't. You'll be pleasantly surprised to discover that when you take care of your spiritual life, all the other parts of your life will fall neatly into place. The famous Christian writer C.S. Lewis observed, "Aim at heaven and you will get earth thrown in."

Mental—It's been said that the mind is a terrible thing to waste. Your mind is like your muscles. Use your muscles, and you will increase in strength. Use your mind, and you increase in your mental capabilities. God wants you to "be transformed by the renewing of your *mind*" so that you can know His will and choose to do it (Romans 12:2).

How can you develop your mind? The simplest and best way is to *read*. It's as easy as that! But we must read with purpose and discernment.

A central scripture that points us to the importance of the mind and its focus is Romans 12:2: "Do not be conformed to this world, but be transformed by the renewing of your mind, that you may prove what is that good and acceptable and perfect will of God." Follow me through these words:

God first gives a warning—"Do not be conformed to this world." Whether you realize it or not, your world—your society, your environment—is at work squeezing you into its mold, its image. You are bombarded every minute of every day with the world's influences. God knows the evil and powerful pull of this world, so He warns us to watch out and be aware of what could happen.

God next gives a choice—"Be transformed." I love to say, "A problem defined is a problem half solved." So now that we know what we're facing (the pressure of the world), we have a choice. We can choose to continue on our merry way, to compromise our beliefs and biblical standards and be conformed into a mirror image of the world around us. Or we can choose to be changed— to be transformed, which in the original Greek text of Scripture means "metamorphosis." Metamorphosis is what happens when a creepy-looking larva changes into a beautiful monarch butter-fly. This spectacular change, this transformation, is what God desires for us. So the question now is, "How?"

God gives a solution—"By the renewing of your mind." You are transformed as your mind is renewed or your thinking is changed through the study and meditation of Scripture. It's obvi-ous that the best way to renew your mind is to feed continually upon the truths of God's Word. As you read, study, memorize, and meditate on God's Word, the Holy Spirit changes your atti-tude, thinking, and ultimately your actions.

God then gives the result—"That you may prove what is that good and acceptable and perfect will of God." With God's Word in your heart and mind, you will be able to "distinguish good form evil" (Hebrews 5:15 NIV), right from wrong—to recog-nize, choose, and live God's will.

In the Bible (and throughout the history of Christianity) mental development always starts with simply reading and study-ing the Bible. So make the Bible a priority. Use your mind in the best way and on the best content. The more you read your Bible and other Christian books, the more you will grow both spiritually and mentally.

Physical—I grew up with three brothers and a dad who had been a football player and coach. They were forever quoting Vince Lombardi, one of the greatest head coaches of the Green

Bay Packers. One favorite was, "Fatigue makes cowards of us all." This legendary coach knew that, as 1 Timothy 4:8 says, "physical training is of some value" (NIV).

To help you make better choices in the physical area of your life, here are three truths from God's Word:

—your body is a *stewardship* from God,

—your body is the *temple* of the Holy Spirit, and

—your body is meant to *glorify* God (1 Corinthians 6:19-20).

It's obvious God cares about your body and health. Therefore you must choose to take good care of yourself physically. Here are some suggestions:

Watch out for sin—Psalm 32:3-5 tells us what happened to David's physical health when he failed to confess his sin. His body suffered, his bones wasted away, he felt weighed down day and night, and his strength was sapped.

Walk by the Spirit—One "fruit of the Spirit" you enjoy when you are walking in obedience to God's Spirit is "self-control" (Galatians 5:22-23). Self-control enables you to take better care of yourself.

Weigh yourself every day—If the arrow is pointing in the wrong direction, then go in the *right* direction by following the next few suggestions.

Watch what you eat—The apostle Paul said to "discipline" your body (1 Corinthians 9:27). One obvious way to do this is to watch both the quality and quantity of the food you take in (Daniel 1:12-15).

Exercise regularly—You don't have to buy a membership to a local gym and pump iron for hours each day. But maybe you can commit to walking with a friend or your husband—or take the baby out in the stroller. After all, bodily exercise is profitable (1 Timothy 4:8).

Mind your stewardship—The Bible makes it clear that you are not your own, and neither is your body. You were bought with a price—a high price!—by Jesus Christ. So work at being a good steward of it (1 Corinthians 6:19-20).

Win the battle—One of the apostle Paul's secrets to his remarkable ministry and his lasting impact is found in this declaration regarding his body: "I...make it my slave" (1 Corinthians 9:27 NIV). Paul viewed his body as an opponent that had to be conquered at all costs—or else. What are you doing to win the battle for your body? As observed by former President Harry S. Truman, "In reading about the lives of great men, I found that the first victory they won was over themselves...self-discipline with all of them came first."

Social—This section is not talking about your party life. No, it's about your relationships and friendships. The choices you make in this priority area of your life are so key that I've already devoted a whole chapter to it. But here are a few more thoughts on the subject!

You and I are in constant contact with people—at home, at work, at church, in the community...and the list goes on. But you need to be careful that you are not guilty of having too many of the wrong kinds of friends and not enough of the right kinds of friends.

So how do you determine the level of importance of these contacts? In other words, how do you prioritize your family, friends, and acquaintances? To make sure you are on the right track in your social life, consider the four different types or levels of people or relationships that make up your life:

> Level 1: Your family—After your relationship with Christ, your family is your top priority. Never sacrifice your relationship with your family for any lesser relationships. Christ said, "What will it profit a man if he gains the whole world and forfeits his soul?" (Matthew 16:26 NASB). When it comes to my family, I apply Christ's words in a slightly different way: "What will it profit a *woman* to gain the whole world and lose her *family*?" Your family should be precious to you. Therefore you should be making choices that affirm they are your top priority. Even after your children are grown and gone, they are still Number One.

> Level 2: Your friends—Friends are a gift from the Lord, and you should be cultivating friendships with other women, especially those who will encourage you in your faith and give you solid advice. The Bible says, "As iron sharpens iron, so one person sharpens another" (Proverbs 27:17 NIV). That's the kind of friends you need—people who will have a sharpening influence on you.

> What does such a friendship look like? Earlier we looked at Jonathan and David, whose friendship gives us a model to follow. These two men had these things in common—they...

> assented to the same authority,
> knew the same God,
> were going the same way,
> longed for the same things,
> dreamed mutual dreams,
> yearned for the same experiences of holiness and
>   worship, and
> strengthened and encouraged one another in
>   God.

Level 3: Your workmates—You may work alongside others every day. So you will want to make an effort to build relationships with your workmates. The more closely you let them observe your words and actions, the more clearly they will see the image of Jesus stamped on your life. Remember, no contact equals no impact!

And be especially careful in the level of your inter-action with the men at work. To paraphrase a proverb, Don't play with fire (Proverbs 6:27-29).

Level 4: Your neighbors and strangers—Be friendly with everyone you encounter. Give a smile, a word of encour-agement, a helping hand. Show others the love of Christ. And especially be a good neighbor. The same is true for neighbors as for workmates—no contact equals no impact.

When it comes to your social life, be willing to go to the ends of the earth, if needed, to find those relationships that will either propel you forward or pull you up. And conversely, avoid at all costs (like the proverbial plague!) anyone who would pull you down (1 Corinthians 15:33).

Charting a Course for Your Life

Yes, August 31, 1974, was a red-letter day for me. It sent my life into warp speed…and in the right direction. Things have been fast and furious, but in a good way. I could have chosen to go off in a lot of different directions. In fact, that describes what my life was like before I became a Christian. But since that day I have been choosing to focus on what really matters. I have a purpose that goes well beyond me—way beyond me.

The goals I chose took me from being a receiver to being a resource. You see, in the past, my selfish desires were just that—selfish. But as I began to focus and plan my life for the glory of God and according to His Word, I found that I wanted to serve and help my family and others, to be a resource for God in their lives.

Before you move on to the next chapter and finish looking at the eight priority areas of your life, give some thought to writing some goals for yourself. It's never too late to start. Once you take this major step, you will discover that:

> Goals help define the purpose of your life.
>
> Goals help develop a set of priorities for your life.
>
> Goals help determine a focus for your life.
>
> Goals help drive each day of your life.

God's Guidelines for Making Right Choices...
Choosing Your Priorities (Part 1)

These guidelines will help you proceed through your day, confident that you are seeking to make the right choices.

~ *Your spiritual life*—"What does the LORD require of you but to do justly, to love mercy, and to walk humbly with your God?" (Micah 6:8).

~ *Your spiritual life*—"Walk in the Spirit, and you shall not fulfill the lust of the flesh" (Galatians 5:16).

~ *Your mental life*—"The fear of the Lord is the beginning of knowledge" (Proverbs 1:7 NASB).

~ *Your mental life*—"Incline your ear to wisdom, and apply your heart to understanding" (Proverbs 2:2).

~ *Your physical life*—"Bodily exercise profits a little, but godliness is profitable for all things, having promise of the life that now is and of that which is to come" (1 Timothy 4:8).

~ *Your social life*—"A man who had friends must himself be friendly" (Proverbs 18:24).

13

Practicing Your Priorities,
Part 2

Be diligent to present yourself approved to God,
a worker who does not need to be ashamed.
—2 Timothy 2:15

t lasted only two hours, but when it was over, I had a tangible hard-copy set of guidelines that would assist me in the choices I would be making for the rest of my life. I'm talking about that red-letter day I described in the last chapter.

Well, writing those goals was the easy part. Next followed the years of purposefully choosing to practice them! You see, your life is a stewardship. You have responsibilities, roles, and commitments to manage faithfully. And goals hold you accountable in a very visible way to a life that is meant to honor God. Once I put on paper what I believed God wanted me to do (and what I dreamed of doing for Him), I was then duty-bound to live out those prioritites. I, like Timothy in the scripture above, was being challenged to present myself to God as a good manager of the life He had given me.

My heart's desire is to be a woman who can give a positive account to God—and I'm sure you feel the same way. And then you wonder, *How can I do my best to be more diligent?* That's where seeking God's will comes in. Pray Jesus' prayer, "Not My will, but Your will be done." Then, as you begin to understand from Scripture the priorities that God has outlined for you, you'll be able to start setting goals that will move you along the path to fulfilling God's will. That's what it means to be a workman that is approved by God.

Remember, as important as it is to understand God's plan for your days and years and set goals that are in line with His plan, it's equally important that you make daily choices to live out His will. Once you've set your goals, you can then begin to live them out.

We've been analyzing eight areas of life that call for goals— and so far we've looked at the spiritual, mental, physical, and social areas of our lives. Now let's look at the final four areas: vocational, financial, family, and ministry.

Eight Areas of Life that Call for Goals

Vocational—For some women, their vocation is being a stay-at-home mom and wife. For others, their vocation involves working at home (like I do as a writer) or out in the workplace. Whether in the home or the workplace, the Bible has guidelines for you to follow. God wants you to do all your work in a way that glorifies Him (1 Corinthians 10:31). You do this by:

> —striving for excellence (Colossians 3:23-24)
>
> —being content (1 Timothy 6:8)
>
> —submitting to your employer (Ephesians 6:5-8)
>
> —being a servant to others (Galatians 5:13)

Put simply, the quality of your work will be outstanding if you do your work with all your heart, as if you were working for the Lord. Whether in the home or outside of it, "whatever you do, do it heartily, as to the Lord and not to men...for you serve the Lord Christ" (Colossians 3:23-24).

Financial—This can be a sticky area for married couples. Hopefully you are making your financial choices together. But married or not, first up for managing your finances is planning a budget. Then follows the responsibility of making choices that enable you to live within that budget. Your budget will help make your choices very clear. Should you buy that pair of designer jeans or not? What does the budget say? It might tell you no!

And then there's the all-important choice about giving to God. It's true—and sobering—to realize that everything you have has been entrusted to you by God. And He asks us to give some back. The Old Testament tells you—and all believers—to "honor the LORD with your possessions, and with the firstfruits of all your increase." The New Testament also advises us to "lay something aside" regularly and to "purpose in [your] heart" to give to the needs in the church "not grudgingly or of necessity; for God loves a cheerful giver."[31]

Two disciplines—giving *and* saving—have served our family well over the years. Because we have some money set aside in a savings account, we are better prepared for uncertain times and emergencies. (Believe me, we've had to dip into the savings during many an uncertain time!)

Here are some suggestions for handling your finances God's way. You'll notice the spiritual thread that intertwines even your financial life.

Balance—The writer of Proverbs asked God to give him "neither poverty nor riches, but give me only my daily bread" (30:8-9 NIV). Why? Because "otherwise, I may have too much and disown you and say, 'Who is the LORD?' Or I may become poor and steal, and so dishonor the name of my God." This is a balanced perspective on your personal finances—not too little and not too much.

Trust—One of my biggest problems (and I'm sure you can identify) is trust. I wonder, *Can I trust God with my life and my finances?* Jesus gives us the answer: "Do not worry about your life, what you will eat or what you will drink; nor about your body, what you will wear" (Matthew 6:25). The writer of Proverbs gives this admonition: "Trust in the LORD with all your heart, and lean not on your own understanding" (Proverbs 3:5). Thank God regularly that you can trust Him, Creator of all things, with your finances.

Maturity—How would you respond if I said that your checkbook reveals where your heart is? That the way you handle your money is an indicator of your focus and spiritual maturity? Well, it's true. So take a look at your checkbook or credit card statement. What does it show? Money frequently spent on pleasures, hobbies, and personal things? Or money frequently given to God for His work? Always remember that...

> —How you use your finances reveals who you serve.
>
> —You cannot serve both God and money (Matthew 6:24).
>
> —The focus of your finances reveals the focus of your heart (Matthew 6:21).

Never forget that the money you have is not even your money. It's *God's* money, and you and I are simply stewards of it.

Contentment—When it comes to your finances, the apostle Paul was able to say, "I have learned the secret of being content in any and every situation" (Philippians 4:12 NIV). Try saying *no* to yourself more frequently in the "things" department. Try being content with what you have. Try being happy about what other people have. Try being content with "food and clothing" only (1 Timothy 6:8)—and try being content with "godliness" (verse 6). Now that, my friend, is "great gain" in both the financial department and in the spiritual department (verse 8).

Budgeting—When you choose to make and follow a budget, you are exhibiting wisdom and exercising "self-control," a fruit of the Spirit (Galatians 5:22). A budget is a battle plan for curbing the lure of our needs-driven society. A budget helps you see clearly how to manage God's resources. Ask any financial adviser what the first step to financial freedom is. You'll probably hear, "Make a budget...and keep it!"

7. *Family*—I can't express strongly enough that family is your Number One priority after your relationship with God. And if you are married, loving your family starts with your husband. When you deliberately choose to focus your love and attention on him, all your other family relationships will fall into place.

If you have children, be what I call a "fierce" mom—a mom who cares, really cares. Commit yourself to doing the loving, leading, teaching, training, even disciplining. Your children should receive the greatest investment of your time and energy—and prayers.

And there are more priority people. Don't forget the in-laws. As your husband's parents, they go high up on your list of priority people. Do whatever it takes to be a loving, attentive, respectful daughter-in-law.

Also, married or not, you have parents and/or step-parents. Honor them. Pull out the stops on your love for them. Spend time with them, and stay in touch. Most women are a sister—big or little—to someone, which is another wonderful role that deserves your time. And, one of my favorites is watching aunts befriend, spoil, spend time, and influence their nieces and nephews. God has given you a rich list of relatives—family—to love and cherish and bless. And even if you find yourself without family, you have God's added blessing of the entire family of God.

Ministry—What does a godly woman do? Like those in the Bible did, she serves! Women helped Jesus, a woman named Dorcas helped widows, and the women of the church in Ephesus helped care for the needs of those in the church.[32] Maybe you are unsure of your area of ministry expertise and giftedness, but until you know, serve your heart out. Serve anyone and everyone who crosses your path. The good news is that service and good works is a ministry you can have right now. There is no training required to be a servant. So choose to serve! As the Bible exhorts, "As we have opportunity, let us do good to all, especially those who are of the household of faith" (Galatians 6:10).

Beyond the good works of your physical service, seek to discover what the Bible calls "spiritual gifts" (1 Corinthians 12:1-11). These "gifts" are spiritual enablements given to Christians through the ministry of the Holy Spirit (verse 7).

How can you know what your spiritual gifts are? Begin by serving. Be faithful, and be growing spiritually. As you serve you will discover your areas of giftedness. Like physical talents and abilities, spiritual gifts are discerned and developed as they are being used.

Becoming a Woman of Influence

Dear friend, I am thinking of you right now. For the first 28 years of my life I had only three priorities—me, myself, and I! I am pleading with you, please don't drift through life without a course, a compass, or a cause. Others are depending on your presence and influence in their lives. Take aim. Make the choice to set your own goals. Point your life and activities toward the mark of God's high calling on your life. Know where you are going and how to get there. If tending to your God-given priorities is a choice you are willing to make, then you will most definitely have an impact.

As we wrap up these two chapters on choosing to practice your priorities, I can't help but think of a principle taught by the ancient Greeks. They were concerned with the development of the whole person. They saw a man or woman as less than whole if any part of the body, soul, or spirit was undeveloped.

I think we can safely say that choosing to set goals and practicing God's plan for these eight areas of life we've just examined will make you not only a whole woman, but a woman of influence with a lasting impact. Here are a few choices you can make to get you started:

> Choose to take time to set some goals in each of these eight areas of life. How about today?

> Choose to do several activities each day that will help you reach your goals in these areas of life. Put them on your daily to-do list.

Choose to review your goals often, especially when you pray.

Choose to keep your focus on what really matters—your priorities.

God's Guidelines for Making Right Choices... Choosing Your Priorities (Part 2)

These guidelines will help you proceed through your day, confident that you are seeking to make the right choices.

~ *Your vocational life*—"Whatever you do, do all to the glory of God" (1 Corinthians 10:31).

~ *Your financial life*—"You were faithful over a few things, I will make you ruler over many things" (Matthew 25:21).

~ *Your financial life*—"It is required in stewards that one be found faithful" (1 Corinthians 4:2).

~ *Your family life*—"She watches over the ways of her household, and does not eat the bread of idleness" (Proverbs 31:27).

~ *Your family life*—"Honor your father and mother" (Ephesians 6:2).

~ *Ministry*—"[Teach] the young women" (Titus 2:4).

14

Counting on God to Lead You

Trust in the LORD with all your heart,
and lean not on your own understanding;
in all your ways acknowledge Him,
and He shall direct your paths.
—PROVERBS 3:5-6

We have come a long way, haven't we? When you take a minute to think about your choices and how serious their consequences can be, it's rather sobering, isn't it? And I hope and pray that you have received the message loud and clear about the importance of taking care to make right choices. That's why I have spent so much time in this book laying out what the Bible says about the decisions you must make.

There is no quick and easy formula that I or anyone else can give you to completely prepare you for the specifics of making right choices. There are just too many variables and circumstances that can only be evaluated by you as you make your individual choices. But without some guidelines, your decision-making process can begin to feel a bit like throwing darts at a dartboard, or being overwhelmed by the multitude of choices at the world's largest buffet. It could all seem so hopeless. But with a few guidelines right out of God's Word in hand, you can determine how to make better choices.

You see, the right choices you make are an outgrowth of a life that has been infused with the inner strength that comes from living by the principles found in the Bible. And of course, making right choices—choices that honor God—requires you to stay close to God.

Just because we know the guidelines for making right choices doesn't mean we won't make mistakes along the way. Of course there will be some slipups. If you think back on the times you've made a wrong choice, chances are you may realize they took place at times when your heart was not burning hot for Jesus. In contrast, when you are walking close to the Lord, you are far more likely to make better choices, good choices—even the best choices. The condition of your relationship with God has a dramatic effect on the choices you make.

Knowing the Right Choices to Make

How can you keep your love for Jesus burning hot so that you are more consistent when it comes to making right choices? Proverbs 3:5-6 has been a huge help for me in making decisions, whether they are the split-second on-the-spot decisions, or those choices that call for the longer, more intense process of regular, diligent prayer. This is a pair of verses you've probably heard and loved...and maybe even memorized. Let God use these well-known verses to lead you to right choices—to direct your steps as He leads you on the right path, His path.

Trust in the LORD with all your heart (verse 5)—Do you ever feel like there's no one you can trust or who understands what you're feeling when you have an important decision to make? It's awful feeling so alone! No one seems to relate. Your friends are of little or no help. You feel like the weight of the world is on your shoulders. You half-pray, "If only there was someone I could talk to…someone I could trust with my problems and decisions…"

And when your list comes up empty, you decide there isn't anyone who can help you. So, you make your choice alone, without any input from others. Sometimes your choice is okay. But other times it leads to disaster.

You can already guess what I'm about to say next, can't you? Yes! There *is* someone you can trust 100 percent with 100 percent of the choices you must make. That someone is God. And God knows 100 percent of the time what is 100 percent best for you. He's a better judge of what's right and what you need and what's good or harmful for you than you are. In fact, He's the best!

Well, my friend, in every choice you make, from the small ones to the monumental ones, you can completely trust and believe that God can—and will—help you make the right choice. That's where trusting the Lord "with all your heart" (verse 5) comes in. That means without reserve—with 100 percent or "all" of your heart. You can trust Him for the salvation of your soul, and you can trust Him to direct your life.

Lean not on your own understanding (verse 5)—God isn't asking you to give up your ability to think and reason. But He *is* asking you to listen to the wisdom of His Word, to your conscience, and the prompting of His Spirit, along with wise counsel.

I can testify to how easy it is to make wrong choices. You probably know the scene yourself. You wanted what you wanted. And you were listening to the wrong people—to everyone but God. You were totally excluding God (whether intentionally or not) and the resources He has given you (like His Word and prayer) to help with the choices you were making: In short, you were leaning on your own understanding.

As I'm thinking about this all-too-familiar scenario, I'm seeing clearly why God tells us—yes, tells us point blank in a "do not" statement—"lean not to your own understanding." In a world centered on self, God is asking us to develop a healthy distrust of self. As hard as it is for us to admit, we are simply not capable of guiding ourselves. This is what the prophet Jeremiah was communicating when he declared, "O Lord, I know the way of man is not in himself; it is not in man who walks to direct his own steps" (Jeremiah 10:23).

In all your ways acknowledge Him (verse 6)—How do you acknowledge the presence of a friend? You call out to her. You wave. You flash a smile and send out a greeting. You rush to her and are glad to see her. Acknowledging God is similar. He's always there, "with you wherever you go" (Joshua 1:9). So, make sure you're always aware of Him and His presence. The best way to do that is to pray. Call out to Him. Rush to Him. Bring your every decision to the Lord in prayer. Turn to Him for help with your choices. Every one of them is important to Him...and should be to you too. He's wanting you to realize your need for His divine advice. Just pray with a sincere heart, "Lord, what would You have me do?"

He shall direct your paths (verse 6)—Trusting God and putting Him at the center of your life moves you closer to Him, to receiving His guidance in the choices you have to make. Proverbs 3:6 reveals that your job is to acknowledge God in everything and seek His will. Then His job is to direct and guide you—to make your paths obvious and straight. One of my favorite books on the Proverbs summarizes Proverbs 3:6 with these serious challenges:

Every area of our lives must be turned over to His control. We must have no will of our own, only a single pure desire to know His will and to do it.

If these conditions are met, the promise is that God will provide the necessary guidance. He may do it through the Bible, through the advice of godly Christians, through the marvelous converging of circumstances, through the inward peace of the Spirit, or through a combination of these. But if we wait, He will make the guidance so clear that to refuse would be positive disobedience.[33]

Once you make your right choices, you must once again trust God. You must count on Him to clear out the roadblocks, remove the hurdles, and enable you to move forward toward His will. And because you'll be making the right choices, you'll be enjoying life more and suffering less. How cool is that?

The Blessings of Trusting God

As you read each of the passages below, you may want to grab your pen and circle the blessing and results of trusting in the Lord with all your heart.

This is what the LORD says: "Stand in the ways and see, and ask for the old paths, where the good way is, and walk in it; then you will find rest for your souls" (Jeremiah 6:16).

"I know the plans I have for you," declares the LORD, "plans to prosper you and not to harm you, plans to give you hope and a future" (Jeremiah 29:11 NIV).

Seek first the kingdom of God and His righteousness, and all these things shall be added to you
(Matthew 6:33).

Do not conform to the pattern of this world, but be
transformed by the renewing of your mind. Then
you will be able to test and approve what God's will
is—his good, pleasing and perfect will (Romans
12:2 NIV).

If any of you lacks wisdom, let him ask of God, who
gives to all liberally and without reproach, and it
will be given to him (James 1:5).

Knowing About God's Forgiveness

As you read the verses above, did any lights flash or turn
on in your mind? Were there any revelations? When you think
about decision making and the will of God, it's so simple! All
you have to do is follow God and trust Him with every detail
of your life, and He will gladly help you make the right choices.
(And, of course, we both know that is easier said than done!)

But sometimes there is just one little problem—actually a
big one: your sin. You can try as hard as you can to be obedi-
ent, but from time to time you are sure to slip up. Maybe a little
white lie here and there, a little gossiping, breaking a traffic law.
You know, little things like these. Or maybe you have a slip-up
that's of the huge life-changing sort. Maybe you had an abor-
tion, committed adultery, or knowingly married an unbeliever.

You may be sighing and wondering, *I can't believe I did that.
How will I ever be able to go on? How in the world can I make this
right with God? How could God ever forgive me?*

Well, God in His love comes to the rescue again! As the apostle Paul explains in Ephesians 1:7, "In Him [Jesus] we have redemption through His blood, the forgiveness of sins, according to the riches of His grace." As a Christian, your sins—whether little or large—were forgiven when you received Jesus as Lord and Savior. God forgives, but you and I are to do our part—we are to confess and forsake our sins. As 1 John 1:9 teaches, "If we confess our sins, He is faithful and just to forgive us our sins and to cleanse us from all unrighteousness."

My friend, if you have not received God's forgiveness of your sin, you can. This simple prayer from your heart to God's can transform your life.

> Jesus, I know I am a sinner. I want to repent of my sins and turn and follow You. I believe You died for my sins and rose again victorious over the power of sin and death, and I want to accept You as my personal Savior. Come into my life, Lord Jesus, and help me obey You from this day forward. Amen.

What freedom you have and enjoy as a child of God—the burden of your failure to live for Jesus is lifted! God's forgiveness should leave you sensing the freedom that results when the cleansing power of Jesus washes over you.

It's Time to Move On

Isn't God great? He has given you and me the gift of salvation through His Son that keeps on giving ongoing forgiveness. So the issue for you may be that you are wondering, *How can I move on after I've failed?*

If anyone had a good reason to regret some horrible things he'd done in his life, it was the apostle Paul. Before he met Jesus,

Paul helped in the stoning death of a righteous man named Stephen (Acts 7:59–8:1). He also played a major part in the persecution of Christians (Acts 9:1-2).

Can you imagine how Paul felt when Jesus brought him to his knees and gave him complete and unconditional forgiveness (Acts 9:3-6)? But one thing Paul knew was that he had to move on, to grow and serve God with his whole heart from that day on. No more wasted days! Oh, to be sure, Paul had regrets and deep sorrow for his past actions. But he could also say:

> Forgetting those things which are behind and
> reaching forward to those things which are ahead,
> I press toward the goal for the prize of the upward
> call of God in Christ Jesus (Philippians 3:13-14).

Like Paul, you must make a few more choices. You must choose to accept God's forgiveness for your past. And you must choose to remember His forgiveness every time you are tempted to recall your past failures. And like Paul, you must choose to move on, to forget the past and press on toward the future. When you trust in God's forgiveness, you can face each day and the coming years with excitement and joyful expectation of what God has prepared for you.

Here's an encouraging thought about moving on: If you've strayed and taken the wrong path, you can start walking on a new and right path—God's path—anytime. And even if the consequences are ongoing, God can and will give you the grace to do what is necessary to make things right and help you live with those consequences. You can do everything—including moving on, including turning your life around—through Christ, who gives you His strength (Philippians 4:13).

Trust Him…and move on. An incredible life awaits you!

God's Guidelines for Making Right Choices... Choosing to Count on God

These guidelines will help you proceed through your day, confident that you are seeking to make the right choices.

~ *Always remember that you are known and loved by God*—"Before I formed you in the womb I knew you; before you were born I sanctified you" (Jeremiah 1:5).

~ *Always remember that God's Son died for your sins*—"God demonstrates His own love toward us, in that while we were still sinners, Christ died for us" (Romans 5:8).

~ *Always remember you are accepted by God through His Son*—"To the praise of the glory of His grace, by which He made us accepted in the Beloved" (Ephesians 1:6).

~ *Always remember you are complete in Christ*—"In Him dwells all the fullness of the Godhead bodily; and you are complete in Him, who is the head of all principality and power" (Colossians 2:9-10).

~ *Always remember you are a work in progress and will one day be perfect*—"Being confident of this very thing, that He who has begun a good work in you will complete it until the day of Jesus Christ" (Philippians 1:6).

A Final Word About Choices: Creating a Beautiful Life

In the books I've read that have an epilogue, the events that occur in that add-on chapter entitled "Epilogue" usually take place later in time—six months later, or five years later. It's the author's way of wrapping things up, of tying up all the loose ends and "I wonders" the reader may have with a nice, appealing bow.

Well, here in this epilogue of this book, I want to go *back* in time—back to a choice I had made. I opened this book with a scene of me working in the kitchen when my Jim arrived home from work. (What is it about kitchens that causes everyone to eventually congregate there?) As I said, that was a momentous day—and a momentous choice I made—when Jim and I discussed the merits of me tiptoeing into the waters of teaching the Bible, of testing out this new kind of ministry.

That was a rosy time in my life. I felt like I had everything in order. Thanks to God's Word to me as a wife and mom, I had been working on my marriage and family for a good ten years. There were no flashing lights warning me that any one of my brood was suffering or nearing a calamity. There seemed to be no significant issues in need of my attention.

So, with my husband's encouragement and full support, I said yes to my church's invitation to share a workshop in our newly-formed women's ministry. And, oh, how I grew. And in oh-so-many ways! And how God used that hesitant, whispered, "Yes, Lord," followed quickly by a plea to God with my very next breath, "Lord, help me!"

As you already know, it was a dramatic, but subtle, turning point in my life and ministry.

Well, now let me back up to another scene ten years earlier—to another choice I had made.

I was in the same house, the same kitchen.

Only this incident occurred during my days of darkness—what I now refer to as "the dark days." Yes, I was a Christian, albeit a baby one. But I struggled relentlessly against depression. Even though I lived in sunny Southern California, the inside of our little house on Friar Street was murky. I cried daily as I worked in that kitchen. I cried as I made the beds each day, wishing I could lie down in one of them and pull the covers up over my head, thinking maybe then the grey fog that covered my day and my thoughts would go away.

But, praise God, one day as I stood washing dishes in that kitchen, I fought back. Instead of sliding down the black hole of depression once again, I grasped at one thing I had heard at a recent Christian conference. The speaker had simply stated, "You should all be memorizing Scripture."

With good intentions, I had already purchased a packet of verses designed to help Christians strengthen their faith and trust in God. And even in the clutter that defined my home—and homemaking—I knew where that little packet was. I dried my hands, grabbed the tiny bundle out of a cubbyhole in my roll-top desk, ripped off the cellophane wrapping, and pulled out Verse #1.

Back in the kitchen, I propped the little card up on the windowsill over the sink and began hiding that one verse in my heart. I said the verse out loud, then broke it down into phrases, and kept repeating those phrases to myself one by one as I finished up the dishes.

If I had known more about the Bible and its contents, I might have looked at that verse—which happened to be Philippians 4:8—and thought, *My, that's a l-o-n-g verse! And it looks a little complicated. I think I'll choose another one, a short one. After all, I'm just a beginner at this.*

But no. Ignorance is bliss. I continued marching my way through that verse. And without any drumroll or lightning-and-thunder theatrics, that verse became my breakthrough verse. Yes, this verse contains eight qualifications God desires for our thoughts to meet. And I struck gold on the first quality, which the apostle Paul had written to friends who were suffering: "Finally, brethren, whatever things are true…think on these things" (KJV).

As I went over and over—and over!—these eight words—"whatever things are true…think on these things"—God used His Word to show me the way through my darkness and out of my dark thoughts. I was to think only on what is true.

All I can say is I'm soooo glad I chose to reach for that life-line, that little life-saving packet of verses that led to a monu-mentally life-changing explosion in my Christian growth and my spiritual mental health. To this day, I still recite this first-ever memorized verse when I find my thoughts headed downward.

I'm sure you're not surprised to learn that I then made another choice—to continue to memorize Scripture as a habit for life.

Now let's fast-forward to today. At this season in my life, Jim and I reside part-time in the Seattle area, near one of our daughters, whose family lives in Vancouver, BC, and part-time in Hawaii, near our other daughter, whose family lives in Honolulu, where her US Navy husband is based.

Of course, if you've read any of my other books, you know how Jim and I adore living in Washington, hidden and lost among our giant cedar, fir, and pine trees and looking out over the Hood Canal while working at warp speed, taking in the majestic and eternally snowcapped Mount Rainier, catching glimpses of eagles soaring by, salmon jumping, and seals cruising. We're surrounded by unbelievable beauty in a tranquil setting—perfect for two writers!

But Hawaii couldn't be more opposite. It is the land of green, craggy volcanic slopes, mist on the mountains, abundant sun, warm tropical breezes, swaying palms, white sandy beaches, and a variegated blue ocean lined with white-capped tumbling surges of surf. Like Washington, Hawaii is also a place of peace, offering a more laid-back "island style" of living—also perfect for two creative writers!

Needless to say, we have been learning much about Hawaiian culture and customs. The one I'm thinking about right now is the tradition of greeting guests who are arriving to the Islands with a lei. A lei is a flower-woven garland placed over the head and around the neck of a special recipient, always followed with a hug, a kiss on the cheek, and an "Aloha" greeting, which means, "Hello and welcome."

It's such a delightful, loving tradition that Jim and I have adopted it when welcoming friends and family who arrive for an island visit. On the way to the Honolulu Airport, one slight turn to the left takes us to a famous row of outdoor lei stands. Inside these stalls, island women sit all day with baskets of fresh-cut exotic tropical blossoms at their feet. A lei is a work of art and is never quickly or thoughtlessly slapped together. Each single blossom is chosen for a purpose—to add a special color, to compliment another color, to indicate whether the lei is for a male or female, to interject fragrance, or to form an intricate pattern.

My friend, think about yourself. I want you to carry this imagery of creating an intricate lei in your mind as you go through your days of decision-making. I want you to think of yourself as making your choices as carefully, deliberately, and purposefully as these ladies choose each individual blossom that they sew into their awe-inspiring flower leis.

I know your days are beyond hectic. But each choice you make in the midst of chaos has a powerful effect on you and on others. As you walk through life, I want you to picture yourself, quietly sitting before the Lord, pausing as you look over all the options, praying for guidance, and thinking about which "blossom" or choice you will take next to create your most beautiful, breathtaking "lei"—a weaving of a gracious life that reflects God's peace, order, beauty, and blessing. You will be blessed...and so will all those who make up your days and cross your path. Your life will be one that is filled with the beauty and fragrance of the Lord!

> Ho`onani i ka Makua Mau. Âmene.
> (meaning in the Hawaiian language)
> Praise to the Eternal Father. Amen.

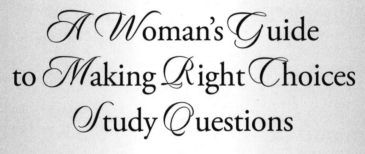

A Woman's Guide
to Making Right Choices
Study Questions

1
Life Is Full of Choices

1. I shared a really significant choice that I made years ago that changed the direction of my life. Pause and think about a similar kind of "I'll never forget" choice you made. How was your life impacted by that choice, and in what way were the priorities of your life redirected?

2. Read again the section titled "Choices Usually Result in Consequences" and author Steve Farrar's story about Jane. How does this real-life account speak to you about the far-reaching magnitude of a single choice?

3. Scan through the section "Looking at Choices Through the Rearview Mirror." Do any of the phrases often included in a woman's story fit your life today? If so, talk it over with God. Admit to Him any wrong choices. Then ask for His wisdom to help you make right choices starting immediately. To help turn things around, complete this sentence: "Today I will...

4. Read through the Bible verses listed below and think about the choices made by these women. Share what you learn from the choice made by each, and the lesson to your heart.

Eve (Genesis 3:1-6)—

Lot's wife (Genesis 13:10-11)—

Mary, the mother of Jesus (Luke 1:26-38)—

Mary, who sat at Jesus' feet (Luke 10:38-42)—

5. As stated in the chapter, choices are a matter of your will. You get to decide what you will or won't do, how you will or won't act. What are you struggling with or facing today—your Number One challenge for the day? Before you meet it head-on, determine in advance...

What you will and won't do—

How you will and won't act—

What you will and won't say—

6. Then write out a prayer for God's help and guidance to make the right choices for this one day!

2
Seven Steps for Making Right Choices

1. Step 1 for those moments when your day falls apart is to stop—quickly! That's because the surest way to make a wrong choice is to rush before reasoning. Looking back over the last few days, what serves as an example of a time when it would have been good for you to stop but didn't? What valuable lesson or two did you learn from that?

2. The second step is to wait. Try to think of at least three benefits of waiting rather than reacting without thinking:

    •

    •

    •

3. The third step for making right choices is to search the Scriptures. In what two or three areas do you find yourself "tripping up" fairly regularly? Do you have any Scripture passages you can turn to for help in those areas—such as Philippians 4:6 for those times when you are anxious? Try to find a passage for each of the two or three problems you face most frequently. Write the Scripture references below, then start making a practice of turning to them when you need help.

4. Step 4 is to pray. Too often when we look for help or solutions, the last thing we do is pray, when it should be the first thing. In Matthew 26:39, we read about Jesus immediately before His arrest and crucifixion. What action did He take? And what was His request? Why should this be our request as well?

5. Step 5 is to seek counsel. What are the qualities you would look for in someone whom you approach for counsel? Can you share an example of when another woman's counsel was immensely helpful to you?

6. Next is to make a decision. By now you've consulted the Bible, sought God in prayer, and asked others for counsel. How will all this help shape the choice you ultimately make?

7. Finally, Step 7 is to act on your decision. This may take time to do, but it's well worthwhile. Is there a decision you need to make today? Take time now to walk that decision through the seven steps listed above!

3
Getting a Jump on Your Day

1. What do the first few minutes of a typical morning look like for you? In what areas do you see room for improvement?

2. You've probably heard the saying, "Where there's a will, there's a way." It's true—when you are motivated to get up, you'll make it happen. What are the top motivators you have that give you reason to get up? List them here.

3. Why would writing a schedule the night before help your day go more efficiently?

4. On a scale of 1 to 10, with 10 being the best possible score, how would you rate your time management during the day? How much of an impact do you think the way you spend your first few moments have on the rest of your day?

5. Starting tomorrow, what one step can you take—even if it's a very simple one—that will help improve the way you start your day? Remember, big results begin with small steps!

6. Read through the section "Things to Do Today to Get a Jump on Your Day." Which step in this list is particularly powerful to you right now, and why?

4

Fanning the Flame of Your Heart

1. In what ways would reading your Bible at the beginning of the day make a difference in your day?

2. George Muller wrote, "The vigor of our spiritual life will be in exact proportion to the place held by the Bible in our life and thoughts." According to Psalm 19:7-11, what are some ways that reading your Bible can bring vigor to your spiritual life?

3. Can you share about a specific time that Scripture provided you with much-needed wisdom in the midst of a crisis?

4. Reviewing page 55, what is wrong with the reasoning, *I just don't have time to stop and spend time with God*?

5. Under the section "Count Your Blessings," look again at the ways the Bible can bring blessing to you. Which one or two is especially relevant to you right now, and why? Take some time now to thank God for what He has provided to you in Scripture.

6. Read through the section "God's Guidelines for Making Right Choices...About Getting into the Bible." Which truth in this list is particularly powerful to you right now, and why?

5
Powering Up for
a Great Day

1. God is available to hear your prayers 24/7. What does that
   tell you about the extent of His care for you? And in what
   ways does that knowledge comfort you?

2. Look over the section "10 Reasons We Don't Pray." What
   two or three excuses for not praying do you relate to most?
   What action steps can you take to make these excuses less
   of a problem?

3. "Any prayer is better than no prayer." One very helpful way to overcome a lack of discipline when it comes to prayer is to make a commitment—and keep it! For me, it started with setting my kitchen timer for five minutes. What can you do, starting today, to make prayer a regular habit, even if it's just one small step?

4. A great way to recognize the power of prayer is to keep track of your prayer requests in a notebook or diary. Then, as time goes by and God does His work in your life, you can go back and marvel over how He has answered your petitions to Him. Again, starting small is better than doing nothing at all! You can start right here by writing the names of others in need of prayer, and noting any specific concerns you want to lift up to God.

5. As Philippians 4:6-7 says, we are to pray rather than worry. What is causing anxiety in your heart today? Take time to pray about it right now. And what does verse 7 say will happen when you've truly let go of your concern and placed it in God's more-than-competent hands?

6. Read through the section "God's Guidelines for Making Right Choices…About Prayer." Which truth in this list is particularly powerful to you right now, and why?

6
Living More Like Jesus

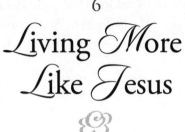

1. With help from the section "What It Means to Walk in the Spirit," state in your own words what it means to walk in the Spirit.

2. Among the fruit of the Spirit is joy. As stated on page 87, what is the distinction between spiritual joy and emotional happiness? What does joy focus on, and what does emotional happiness focus on?

3. Read through John Wesley's "rules" regarding the principle of doing everything (see page 91). If you were to carry this out for a person close to you (such as your husband, your children, a dear friend)—for just one day—how might that look?

4. What does self-control choose to do? In what areas of your life would you like to follow the Spirit's leading and exercise more self-control?

5. It's not possible to walk in sin and walk in the Spirit at the same time. As Galatians 5:16 says, "Walk in the Spirit, and you shall not fulfill the lust of the flesh." Read 1 John 1:9. Is there any sin presently in your heart that you need to surrender to God? Take time now to pray and confess it to the Lord so that you can make the choice to walk in the Spirit!

6. Read through the section "God's Guidelines for Making Right Choices...Living More Like Jesus." Which truth in this list is particularly powerful to you right now, and why?

7

Making the Most of Your Time

1. Read Ephesians 5:15-16. When you think in terms of wasted time, what immediately comes to your mind? What can you replace these time-wasters with?

2. According to Psalm 90:12, what is the result when we number our days?

3. On the next page, I've listed some choices you can make right now to make better use of your time. For each one, think of a single action you can take today so you can start redeeming your time more wisely. Again, it's fine to start small. Even just one tiny step in each area will add up and make a big difference!

Choose to do it now—

Choose to make a plan or schedule—

Choose to guard your time with people—

Choose to multiply your activities—

Choose to limit time spent on your computer—

Choose to limit your time on the phone—

Choose your reading material carefully—

Choose the right priority—

4. Read through the section "God's Guidelines for Making Right Choices...Choosing to Value Time." Which truth in this list is particularly powerful to you right now, and why?

Breaking Your Worry Habit

1. What command does Jesus give in Matthew 6:25? For what reason should we obey this command (verse 32)? And what should we do instead (verse 33)?

2. When it comes to worry, Philippians 4:6 offers both a command and a cure. What is the command? What is the cure? What concerns do you have today that you can yield to God right now in prayer?

3. Review the section "Choose Not to Worry." What are some of the benefits you'll enjoy when you turn over every anxiety to God?

4. One of the guidelines for choosing not to worry is "Believe God has your best in mind." In what ways do the following verses confirm this truth?

Deuteronomy 31:6—

Hebrews 4:16—

Nahum 1:7—

Psalm 23:4-5—

5. Read through the section "God's Guidelines for Making Right Choices...Choosing Not to Worry." Which truth in this list is particularly powerful to you right now, and why?

9
Managing Your Friendships

1. While you aren't responsible for what your friends do and don't do to you, you *are* responsible for the kind of friend you are. Why would making the following choices make you a better friend to others?

   Choose to grow closer to the Lord—

   Choose to be yourself—

   Choose to be loyal—

   Choose to be honest—

   Choose to encourage—

   Choose to work at friendships—

2. In what ways could you consider your parents good friends (or if not your parents, perhaps your siblings or other close relatives)? What are a couple key ways you can develop this friendship more?

3. Why do you think Scripture offers warnings about certain kinds of friends to avoid? What are the possible dangers of taking these warnings too lightly?

4. In the "God's Guidelines for Making Right Choices... Choosing Friends" section, I've listed five qualities to look for in good friends. What two or three additional qualities would you say are important to you?

5. Read through the section "God's Guidelines for Making Right Choices...Choosing Your Friends." Which truth in this list is particularly powerful to you right now, and why?

10
$\mathcal{K}$eeping $\mathcal{W}$atch over $\mathcal{W}$hat $\mathcal{Y}$ou $\mathcal{S}$ay

1. One incentive to avoid gossip is to reflect back on how it has hurt you in the past. Think of an instance when another person's poorly chosen words brought pain to you. Based on that example, what can you yourself learn to avoid doing to others?

2. On page 143 I describe three categories of gossip. Let's focus on the last two:

   In what ways do we sometimes rationalize gossip? How might we be able to determine when we are falling into this trap?

Describe how innocent gossip works. Again, what are some ways we might be able to determine whether we are engaging in this?

3. Look at the three T's on pages 145–146. What are some possible guidelines you can place upon yourself to help prevent the possibility your talk might turn into gossip?

4. One tip I give for avoiding gossip is to give words of praise. In a world filled with so much negative talk, you'll stand out as a refreshing difference—and others will enjoy being friends with you! What are some ways you can praise others and be a woman who is *for* other women rather than *against* them?

5. Read through the section "God's Guidelines for Making Right Choices...Choosing Your Words Carefully." Which truth in this list is particularly powerful to you right now, and why?

11
Expanding Your Mind

1. In the section "Learning as a Lifestyle," I list several different ways to look at learning. Which one encouraged you the most? How would you make this real in your life?

2. Read Proverbs 4:5-9. What are some benefits of pursuing wisdom?

3. Think for a moment about your reading choices right now. Are these the best possible choices, or do you see room for improvement? What changes could you make?

4. Read Colossians 3:23-24. If you were to write these verses on an index card and place them on your computer (or a book), how might that change your reading choices? When you make an effort to be mindful of what God's Word says, it will help you to do better at making the best possible choices.

5. When my mother-in-law, Lois, passed away, we could say of her, "She died learning." What kind of legacy would you like to leave to others with regard to learning?

6. Read through the section "God's Guidelines for Making Right Choices...Choosing to Learn." Which truth in this list is particularly powerful to you right now, and why?

12
Practicing Your Priorities,
Part 1

1. In this chapter and the next, I list eight areas of life that call for goals. Below are the first four. In each area, how much thought have you given to setting goals? Rank these on a scale of 1-10, with 1 being no thought at all, and 10 being a lot of thought.

   Spiritual—

   Mental—

   Physical—

   Social—

2. What do you desire to make your Number One goal right now in each area? This may require some thought—but again, it's okay to start small!

   Spiritual—

   Mental—

   Physical—

   Social—

3. Take some time right now to pray about these priorities, asking God to help you make them a reality in your life—not just today, but in the upcoming weeks and months.

4. Read through the section "God's Guidelines for Making Right Choices...Choosing Your Priorities (Part 1)." Which truth in this list is particularly powerful to you right now, and why?

13

$\mathscr{P}$racticing $\mathscr{Y}$our $\mathscr{P}$riorities,

Part 2

1. In this chapter and the previous one, I list eight areas of life that call for goals. Below are the final four. In each area, how much thought have you given to setting goals? Rank these on a scale of 1-10, with 1 being no thought at all, and 10 being a lot of thought.

   Vocational—

   Financial—

   Family—

   Ministry—

2. What do you desire to make your Number One goal right now in each area? This may require some thought—but again, it's okay to start small!

Vocational—

Financial—

Family—

Ministry—

3. Take some time right now to pray about these priorities, asking God to help you make them a reality in your life—not just today, but in the upcoming weeks and months.

4. Read through the section "God's Guidelines for Making Right Choices...Choosing Your Priorities (Part 2)." Which truth in this list is particularly powerful to you right now, and why?

14
Counting on God to Lead You

1. When it comes to making right choices, Proverbs 3:5-6 is a tremendous help. Write out the verses below.

2. Note that verse 5 says you can trust God with *all* your heart. God knows 100 percent of the time what is 100 percent best for you. Why are we sometimes reluctant to place our full trust in Him? When we do that, what are we communicating to Him?

3. Verse 6 assures that when you acknowledge God at all times, He will direct your paths. Can you cite a specific example of when God has guided you in the past? What impact did that have on you?

4. Do you sometimes wonder how God can possibly forgive you? What comfort do you find in 1 John 1:9 with regard to God's forgiveness of you?

5. Read through the section "Guidelines for Making Right Choices…Choosing to Count on God." Which truth in this list is particularly powerful to you right now, and why?

A One-Year Daily Bible Reading Plan

		Genesis
❑	1	1–3
❑	2	4–7
❑	3	8–11
❑	4	12–15
❑	5	16–18
❑	6	19–22
❑	7	23–27
❑	8	28–30
❑	9	31–34
❑	10	35–38
❑	11	39–41
❑	12	42–44
❑	13	45–47
❑	14	48–50
		Exodus
❑	15	1–4
❑	16	5–7
❑	17	8–11
❑	18	12–14
❑	19	15–18
❑	20	19–21
❑	21	22–24
❑	22	25–28
❑	23	29–31
❑	24	32–34
❑	25	35–37
❑	26	38–40

Leviticus

- ❏ 27   1–3
- ❏ 28   4–6
- ❏ 29   7–9
- ❏ 30   10–13
- ❏ 31   14–16

February

- ❏ 1   17–20
- ❏ 2   21–23
- ❏ 3   24–27

Numbers

- ❏ 4   1–2
- ❏ 5   3–4
- ❏ 6   5–6
- ❏ 7   7–8
- ❏ 8   9–10
- ❏ 9   11–13
- ❏ 10   14–15
- ❏ 11   16–17
- ❏ 12   18–19
- ❏ 13   20–21
- ❏ 14   22–23
- ❏ 15   24–26
- ❏ 16   27–29
- ❏ 17   30–32
- ❏ 18   33–36

Deuteronomy

- ❏ 19   1–2
- ❏ 20   3–4
- ❏ 21   5–7
- ❏ 22   8–10
- ❏ 23   11–13
- ❏ 24   14–16
- ❏ 25   17–20
- ❏ 26   21–23

| ❏ 27 | 24–26 |
| ❏ 28 | 27–28 |

March

❏ 1	29–30
❏ 2	31–32
❏ 3	33–34

Joshua

❏ 4	1–4
❏ 5	5–7
❏ 6	8–10
❏ 7	11–14
❏ 8	15–17
❏ 9	18–21
❏ 10	22–24

Judges

❏ 11	1–3
❏ 12	4–6
❏ 13	7–9
❏ 14	10–12
❏ 15	13–15
❏ 16	16–18
❏ 17	19–21

Ruth

| ❏ 18 | 1–4 |

1 Samuel

❏ 19	1–3
❏ 20	4–6
❏ 21	7–9
❏ 22	10–12
❏ 23	13–14
❏ 24	15–16
❏ 25	17–18
❏ 26	19–20

❑ 27	21–23
❑ 28	24–26
❑ 29	27–29
❑ 30	30–31

2 Samuel

❑ 31	1–3

April

❑ 1	4–6
❑ 2	7–10
❑ 3	11–13
❑ 4	14–15
❑ 5	16–17
❑ 6	18–20
❑ 7	21–22
❑ 8	23–24

1 Kings

❑ 9	1–2
❑ 10	3–5
❑ 11	6–7
❑ 12	8–9
❑ 13	10–12
❑ 14	13–15
❑ 15	16–18
❑ 16	19–20
❑ 17	21–22

2 Kings

❑ 18	1–3
❑ 19	4–6
❑ 20	7–8
❑ 21	9–11
❑ 22	12–14
❑ 23	15–17
❑ 24	18–19
❑ 25	20–22
❑ 26	23–25

1 Chronicles

- ❏ 27   1–2
- ❏ 28   3–5
- ❏ 29   6–7
- ❏ 30   8–10

May

- ❏ 1   11–13
- ❏ 2   14–16
- ❏ 3   17–19
- ❏ 4   20–22
- ❏ 5   23–25
- ❏ 6   26–27
- ❏ 7   28–29

2 Chronicles

- ❏ 8   1–4
- ❏ 9   5–7
- ❏ 10   8–10
- ❏ 11   11–14
- ❏ 12   15–18
- ❏ 13   19–21
- ❏ 14   22–25
- ❏ 15   26–28
- ❏ 16   29–31
- ❏ 17   32–33
- ❏ 18   34–36

Ezra

- ❏ 19   1–4
- ❏ 20   5–7
- ❏ 21   8–10

Nehemiah

- ❏ 22   1–3
- ❏ 23   4–7
- ❏ 24   8–10
- ❏ 25   11–13

Esther
- ❏ 26   1–3
- ❏ 27   4–7
- ❏ 28   8–10

Job
- ❏ 29   1–4
- ❏ 30   5–8
- ❏ 31   9–12

June

- ❏ 1   13–16
- ❏ 2   17–20
- ❏ 3   21–24
- ❏ 4   25–30
- ❏ 5   31–34
- ❏ 6   35–38
- ❏ 7   39–42

Psalms
- ❏ 8   1–8
- ❏ 9   9–17
- ❏ 10   18–21
- ❏ 11   22–28
- ❏ 12   29–34
- ❏ 13   35–39
- ❏ 14   40–44
- ❏ 15   45–50
- ❏ 16   51–56
- ❏ 17   57–63
- ❏ 18   64–69
- ❏ 19   70–74
- ❏ 20   75–78
- ❏ 21   79–85
- ❏ 22   86–90
- ❏ 23   91–98
- ❏ 24   99–104
- ❏ 25   105–107
- ❏ 26   108–113
- ❏ 27   114–118

❏ 28	119
❏ 29	120–134
❏ 30	135–142

July

| ❏ 1 | 143–150 |

Proverbs

❏ 2	1–3
❏ 3	4–7
❏ 4	8–11
❏ 5	12–15
❏ 6	16–18
❏ 7	19–21
❏ 8	22–24
❏ 9	25–28
❏ 10	29–31

Ecclesiastes

❏ 11	1–4
❏ 12	5–8
❏ 13	9–12

Song of Solomon

| ❏ 14 | 1–4 |
| ❏ 15 | 5–8 |

Isaiah

❏ 16	1–4
❏ 17	5–8
❏ 18	9–12
❏ 19	13–15
❏ 20	16–20
❏ 21	21–24
❏ 22	25–28
❏ 23	29–32
❏ 24	33–36
❏ 25	37–40
❏ 26	41–43

❑ 27   44–46
❑ 28   47–49
❑ 29   50–52
❑ 30   53–56
❑ 31   57–60

August

❑ 1   61–63
❑ 2   64–66

Jeremiah
❑ 3   1–3
❑ 4   4–6
❑ 5   7–9
❑ 6   10–12
❑ 7   13–15
❑ 8   16–19
❑ 9   20–22
❑ 10   23–25
❑ 11   26–29
❑ 12   30–31
❑ 13   32–34
❑ 14   35–37
❑ 15   38–40
❑ 16   41–44
❑ 17   45–48
❑ 18   49–50
❑ 19   51–52

Lamentations
❑ 20   1–2
❑ 21   3–5

Ezekiel
❑ 22   1–4
❑ 23   5–8
❑ 24   9–12
❑ 25   13–15
❑ 26   16–17

❏ 27	18–20
❏ 28	21–23
❏ 29	24–26
❏ 30	27–29
❏ 31	30–31

September

❏ 1	32–33
❏ 2	34–36
❏ 3	37–39
❏ 4	40–42
❏ 5	43–45
❏ 6	46–48

Daniel

❏ 7	1–2
❏ 8	3–4
❏ 9	5–6
❏ 10	7–9
❏ 11	10–12

Hosea

❏ 12	1–4
❏ 13	5–9
❏ 14	10–14

❏ 15   **Joel**

Amos

❏ 16	1–4
❏ 17	5–9

❏ 18   **Obadiah** and **Jonah**

Micah

❏ 19	1–4
❏ 20	5–7

❏ 21   **Nahum**

❑ 22   **Habakkuk**

❑ 23   **Zephaniah**

❑ 24   **Haggai**

         Zechariah
❑ 25   1–4
❑ 26   5–9
❑ 27   10–14

❑ 28   **Malachi**

         Matthew
❑ 29   1–4
❑ 30   5–7

October

❑ 1   8–9
❑ 2   10–11
❑ 3   12–13
❑ 4   14–16
❑ 5   17–18
❑ 6   19–20
❑ 7   21–22
❑ 8   23–24
❑ 9   25–26
❑ 10   27–28

         Mark
❑ 11   1–3
❑ 12   4–5
❑ 13   6–7
❑ 14   8–9
❑ 15   10–11
❑ 16   12–13
❑ 17   14
❑ 18   15–16

Luke

❏ 19	1–2
❏ 20	3–4
❏ 21	5–6
❏ 22	7–8
❏ 23	9–10
❏ 24	11–12
❏ 25	13–14
❏ 26	15–16
❏ 27	17–18
❏ 28	19–20
❏ 29	21–22
❏ 30	23–24

John

| ❏ 31 | 1–3 |

November

❏ 1	4–5
❏ 2	6–7
❏ 3	8–9
❏ 4	10–11
❏ 5	12–13
❏ 6	14–16
❏ 7	17–19
❏ 8	20–21

Acts

❏ 9	1–3
❏ 10	4–5
❏ 11	6–7
❏ 12	8–9
❏ 13	10–11
❏ 14	12–13
❏ 15	14–15
❏ 16	16–17
❏ 17	18–19
❏ 18	20–21
❏ 19	22–23

| ❏ 20 | 24–26 |
| ❏ 21 | 27–28 |

Romans

❏ 22	1–3
❏ 23	4–6
❏ 24	7–9
❏ 25	10–12
❏ 26	13–14
❏ 27	15–16

1 Corinthians

❏ 28	1–4
❏ 29	5–7
❏ 30	8–10

December

| ❏ 1 | 11–13 |
| ❏ 2 | 14–16 |

2 Corinthians

❏ 3	1–4
❏ 4	5–9
❏ 5	10–13

Galatians

| ❏ 6 | 1–3 |
| ❏ 7 | 4–6 |

Ephesians

| ❏ 8 | 1–3 |
| ❏ 9 | 4–6 |

❏ 10	**Philippians**
❏ 11	**Colossians**
❏ 12	**1 Thessalonians**

❑ 13   **2 Thessalonians**

❑ 14   **1 Timothy**

❑ 15   **2 Timothy**

❑ 16   **Titus** and **Philemon**

              Hebrews
❑ 17   1–4
❑ 18   5–8
❑ 19   9–10
❑ 20   11–13

❑ 21   **James**

❑ 22   **1 Peter**

❑ 23   **2 Peter**

❑ 24   **1 John**

❑ 25   **2, 3 John, Jude**

              Revelation
❑ 26   1–3
❑ 27   4–8
❑ 28   9–12
❑ 29   13–16
❑ 30   17–19
❑ 31   20–22

Notes

1. Steve Farrar, *How to Ruin Your Life by 40,* elec. ed. (Chicago: Moody, 2006).

2. Farrar, *How to Ruin Your Life by 40*, p. 15.

3. Neil S. Wilson, ed., *The Handbook of Bible Application* (Wheaton, IL: Tyndale House, 2000), pp. 86-87.

4. Albert M. Wells, Jr., quoting J.D. Eppinga, *Inspiring Quotations* (Nashville,TN: Thomas Nelson, 1988), p. 166.

5. Curtis Vaughan, ed., citing R.K. Harrington and The Jerusalem Bible, respectively, *The Word—the Bible from 26 Translations* (Gulfport, MS: Mathis Publishers, 1991), p. 1033.

6. Sherwood Eliot Wirt and Kersten Beckstrom, *Topical Encyclopedia of Living Quotations*, quoting Fred Beck (Minneapolis, MN: Bethany House, 1982), p. 177.

7. Roy B. Zuck, *The Speaker's Quote Book* (Grand Rapids: Kregel, 1997), p. 290.

8. Ted W. Engstrom, *Motivation to Last a Lifetime* (Grand Rapids: Zondervan, 1984), p. 45.

9. See 1 Thessalonians 4:11; 1 Timothy 2:2; 1 Corinthians 14:40; Proverbs 21:5; Proverbs 31:27.

10. Roy B. Zuck, *The Speaker's Quote Book*, quoting *Teen Esteem Magazine* (Grand Rapids: Kregel, 1997), p. 165, as quoted in Elizabeth George, *A Young Woman's Guide to Making Right Choices* (Eugene, OR: Harvest House, 2003).

11. Derek Kidner, *The Proverbs* (Downers Grove, IL: InterVarsity Press, 1973), pp. 42-43.

12. John C. Maxwell, *Running with the Giants* (Nashville: Warner Faith, 2002).

13. John Piper, *Don't Waste Your Life* (Wheaton, IL: Crossway, 2003), back cover.

14. "Life Is Sweet" 2012 Calendar, illustrated by Mary Engelbreit (Riverside, NJ: Andrews McMeel Publishing, 2011), August 31.

15. Roy B. Zuck, *The Speaker's Quote Book* (Grand Rapids: Kregel, 1997), p. 30.

16. John MacArthur, Jr., *2 Timothy*, The MacArthur New Testament Commentary (Chicago: Moody Press, 1995), p. 162.

17. *God's Words of Life for Teens* (Grand Rapids: Inspirio, 2000), p. 29.

18. Drawn from Elizabeth George, *The Heart of a Woman Who Prays* (Eugene, OR: Harvest House, 2012), pp. 23-39.

19. Jim George, *The Bare Bones Bible® Handbook* (Eugene, OR: Harvest House, 2006), p. 79.

20. Merrill E. Unger, *Unger's Bible Dictionary* (Chicago: Moody Press, 1972), p. 382.

21. John MacArthur, *Liberty in Christ* (Panorama City, CA: Word of Grace Communications, 1986), p. 88.

22. Arnold A. Dallimore, *Susanna Wesley, the Mother of John Wesley* (Grand Rapids: Baker, 1994), p. 15.

23. Curtis Vaughan, general editor, *The Word—the Bible from 26 Translations*, citing New King James Version, Charles B. Williams Translation in the Language of the People, Twentieth Century New Testament, King James Version, and New English Bible (Gulfport, MS: Mathis Publishers, 1991), p. 1885.

24. Adapted from Elizabeth George, *Cultivating a Life of Character—Judges/Ruth* (Eugene, OR: Harvest House, 2002), p. 134.

25. Joe White and Jim Weidmann, gen. eds., *Spiritual Mentoring of Teens* (Wheaton, IL: Tyndale House, 2001), p. 525.

26. A. Naismith, *12,000 Notes, Quotes, and Anecdotes* (London: Pickering & Inglis, 1975), p. 97.

27. Based on and excerpted from Gene A. Getz, *The Measure of a Woman* (Glendale, CA: Regal Books, 1977), p. 32, as quoted in Elizabeth George, *Growing in Wisdom & Faith—James* (Eugene, OR: Harvest House, 2001), p. 89.

28. *God's Words of Life for Teens* (Grand Rapids: Zondervan, 2000), p. 103.

29. William Peterson, *Martin Luther Had a Wife* (Wheaton, IL: Tyndale House, 1983), p. 27.

30. Allan Petersen, *For Men Only* (Wheaton, IL: Tyndale House Publishers, 1974), p. 24.

31. Proverbs 3:9; 1 Corinthians 16:2; 2 Corinthians 9:7.

32. Luke 8:1-3; 24:1; Acts 9:36; 1 Timothy 5:3-10.

33. William McDonald, *Enjoying the Proverbs* (Kansas City, KS: Walterick Publishers, 1982), p. 24.

Books by Elizabeth George

- Beautiful in God's Eyes
- Breaking the Worry Habit…Forever
- Finding God's Path Through Your Trials
- Following God with All Your Heart
- Life Management for Busy Women
- Loving God with All Your Mind
- A Mom After God's Own Heart
- Quiet Confidence for a Woman's Heart
- Raising a Daughter After God's Own Heart
- The Remarkable Women of the Bible
- Small Changes for a Better Life
- Walking with the Women of the Bible
- A Wife After God's Own Heart
- A Woman After God's Own Heart*
- A Woman After God's Own Heart*
  Deluxe Edition
- A Woman After God's Own Heart*—
  A Daily Devotional
- A Woman After God's Own Heart* Collection
- A Woman After God's Own Heart
  DVD and Workbook
- A Woman's Call to Prayer
- A Woman's Daily Walk with God
- A Woman's Guide to Making Right Choices
- A Woman's High Calling
- A Woman's Walk with God
- A Woman Who Reflects the Heart of Jesus
- A Young Woman After God's Own Heart
- A Young Woman After God's Own Heart—
  A Devotional
- A Young Woman's Call to Prayer
- A Young Woman's Guide to Making
  Right Choices

- A Young Woman's Walk with God

Study Guides

- Beautiful in God's Eyes
  Growth & Study Guide
- Finding God's Path Through Your Trials
  Growth & Study Guide
- Following God with All Your Heart
  Growth & Study Guide
- Life Management for Busy Women
  Growth & Study Guide
- Loving God with All Your Mind
  Growth & Study Guide
- A Mom After God's Own Heart
  Growth & Study Guide
- The Remarkable Women of the Bible
  Growth & Study Guide
- Small Changes for a Better Life
  Growth & Study Guide
- A Wife After God's Own Heart
  Growth & Study Guide
- A Woman After God's Own Heart*
  Growth & Study Guide
- A Woman's Call to Prayer
  Growth & Study Guide
- A Woman's High Calling
  Growth & Study Guide
- A Woman's Walk with God
  Growth & Study Guide
- A Woman Who Reflects the Heart of Jesus
  Growth & Study Guide

Children's Books

- A Girl After God's Own Heart
- God's Wisdom for Little Girls
- A Little Girl After God's Own Heart

Books by Jim George

- 10 Minutes to Knowing the Men and
  Women of the Bible
- The Bare Bones Bible* Facts
- The Bare Bones Bible* Handbook
- The Bare Bones Bible* Handbook for Teens
- A Husband After God's Own Heart

- A Leader After God's Own Heart
- A Man After God's Own Heart
- The Man Who Makes a Difference
- The Remarkable Prayers of the Bible
- A Young Man After God's Own Heart
- A Young Man's Guide to Making Right Choices

Books by Jim & Elizabeth George

- God Loves His Precious Children
- God's Wisdom for Little Boys

- A Little Boy After God's Own Heart

About the Author

Elizabeth George is a bestselling author whose passion is to teach the Bible in a way that changes women's lives. She has more than 7 million books in print, including *A Woman After God's Own Heart*® and *A Woman's Daily Walk with God*.

For information about Elizabeth, her books, and her ministry, and to sign up to receive her daily devotions, and to join her on Facebook and Twitter, visit her website at:

www.ElizabethGeorge.com